D1504953

GREAT
PAPER
QUILLING

GREAT PAPER QUILLING

Mickey Baskett

Sterling Publishing Co., Inc.
New York

PROLIFIC IMPRESSIONS PRODUCTION STAFF:

Editor: Mickey Baskett
Copy: Sylvia Carroll
Graphics: Dianne Miller, Karen Turpin
Styling: Laney Crisp McClure
Photography: Jerry Mucklow
Administration: Jim Baskett

Acknowledgements:
A special thanks to Malinda Johnston at Lake City Craft Company, Nixa, MO 65714 for her generosity in supplying product and for her sharing her expertise on the art of quilling.

Library of Congress Cataloging-in-Publication Data Available

Published by Sterling Publishing Company, Inc.
387 Park Avenue South, New York, N.Y. 10016
Produced by Prolific Impressions, Inc.
160 South Candler St., Decatur, GA 30030
©1999 Prolific Impressions, Inc.
Distributed in Canada by Sterling Publishing
c/o Canadian Manda Group, One Atlantic Avenue, Suite 105
Toronto, Ontario, Canada M6K 3E7
Distributed in Great Britain and Europe by Cassell PLC
Wellington House, 125 Strand, London WC2R 0BB, England
Distributed in Australia by Capricorn Link (Australia) Pty. Ltd.
P.O. Box 6651, Baulkham Hills, Business Centre, NSW 2153 Australia

CONTENTS

A friend hears the song in your heart, and sings it back to you when you've forgotten.

May All of Your Dreams Come True

LEARN THE EASY ART
OF QUILLING

Simply put, Quilling is the art of creating little rolls of paper that blossom into exquisite designs. Who would believe that simple rolls of narrow paper strips could become such intricate and beautiful filigree items such as jewelry, designs for mat frames, decorations for lampshades, or Christmas ornaments?

The origins of paper quilling are actually not known, but the art is believed to be at least 500 years old. However, the oldest known quillwork examples date from the 18th or 19th century. It most likely began with European religious orders, but later was considered an appropriate hobby to fill the time of fashionable ladies. It is thought that feather quills were the tools used around which the paper was rolled.

Quilling was sometimes called "paper filigree," and it is thought to have been inspired by metal filigree as a less expensive alternative. It is far less costly than the precious metal wires used in metal filigree. Indeed, some quilling was even gilded. In those days, some of the items decorated with quilling were baskets, tea caddies, trays, firescreens, furniture, and pictures such as coats of arms and floral designs.

Quilling spread from England to New England in America where it was even taught in some boarding schools. Wall candle sconces were a favorite item to decorate at that time.

For some reason, quilling faded into obscurity in the late 1800's and didn't emerge again until the middle of this century. Like many old-time arts and crafts, it happily came back with more modern tools and materials that take the tedium out of it and leave the fun.

Quilled designs can range from frilly and delicate to bold and modern, and from tiny to rather large, as you will see in this book. Over forty projects given here offer you a variety to choose from and to enjoy making for yourself or for gifts.

QUILLING SUPPLIES

In the olden days, feather quills were likely used as a quilling tool. Today there are two modern quilling tools that do the job more efficiently. In years past, handmade papers were used for quilling. Today, precut quilling paper strips can be purchased in several widths and a variety of colors. There are now two types of quilling boards to aid in making the various shapes. All of these up-to-date supplies make quilling easier and more fun than ever.

QUILLING PAPER

In the past, quillers cut their strips by hand. Happily, today you can find precut and pre-packaged quilling paper in a variety of widths and colors. This paper is also the proper weight and quality to roll and hold its shape well. (For instance, paper that is too lightweight won't spring open, and poor quality paper won't roll well.) The strips are typically 24" long and in widths of 1/8", 1/4", 3/8", and 1/2". Wider or narrower widths are seldom used. They are made but not readily available. Also, strips wider than 3/8" are seldom rolled. Wider strips are usually used for fringed design elements.

Quill Trim is also available. These are papers which are gold or silver on one side and are used to incorporate metallic accents. They are seldom rolled except for fringed flowers and bell shapes.

Parchment quilling paper is also available and gives an entirely different look. This comes in a variety of delicate, pastel colors.

The ends of the strips in the package have been bonded together. When you detach a full-length strip from a multi-strip packet, tear off both the ends to be sure there is no bond remaining on the strip when you roll it. Also, *tear* the strips to the lengths needed rather than cutting them, because a torn end will glue down much more smoothly than a cut end.

When storing your papers, store them by width. Also be careful not to damage them as you search through them for a particular color. One way to store and organize lengths of quilling paper is in handmade cardboard boxes that are approximately 3" x 3" x 25". You can add dividers, if needed, for small quantities of paper. ◠

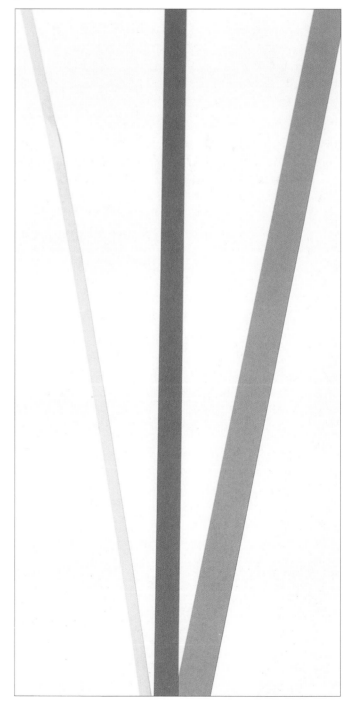

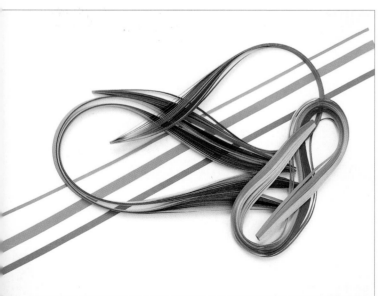

QUILLING TOOLS

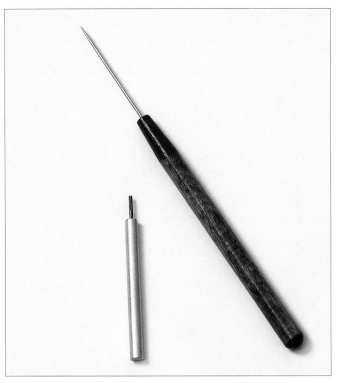

There are two types of quilling tools that make it easy to make the rolls. Both the needle tool and the slotted quilling tool are available at craft stores. Choose either or both, as each has advantages over the other. A hat pin can also be used.

Needle Tool

This is the most popular quilling tool. It is a long needle set into a handle. Shapes are made by rolling paper strips around the needle. The advantage of this tool is that it creates smaller centers to the rolls, especially when the paper is rolled on the tip of the needle (it can also be rolled on the center of the needle).

The needle tool also makes a convenient applicator for the tiny amounts of glue applied to close the shapes and assemble your design. However, be sure to wipe off all glue from the tool with tissue paper. Glue on the tool will cause problems when trying to roll the paper strips.

Slotted Quilling Tool

The slotted tool has a slot at the end into which you insert the end of the paper strip and then roll it. It is the easiest tool to use for learning to quill. However, it leaves a larger hole in the center of the rolled shapes than the needle tool does. The slotted tool is also better for maintaining tension in a strip while making folded roses. The best slotted tool is a metal-handled tool with prongs made of tempered steel which are not easily bent or broken.

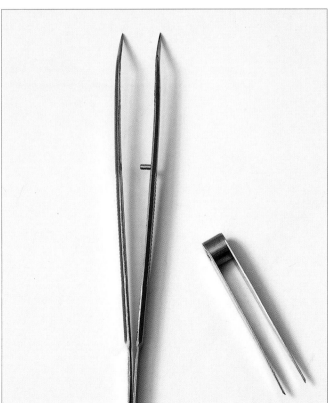

Tweezers

Fine-pointed tweezers help you position tiny shapes during assembly. They are also helpful in adjusting the coils in loose circles and eccentric shapes and rearranging stray fringes. ∽

ADDITIONAL TOOLS

Straight Pins

Use straight pins to hold individual shapes to your handmade quilling board or to hold the centers of eccentric shapes in position on the quilling designer/board while the glue dries. Pins with round plastic heads are easy to grasp and easy to find when dropped.

Clear Drying Glue

Purchase a glue that is colorless when it dries – clear-drying white craft glue. Visible glue on your design can ruin its appearance. Avoid the common white glues used for household repairs and woodworking as they are too thick.

When applying glue, apply a very small amount – never more than is necessary. Apply by dipping the tip of a needle tool or a toothpick into a few drops squeezed onto a small square of paper. Keep your applicator clean by wiping it off with a piece of tissue paper after each use.

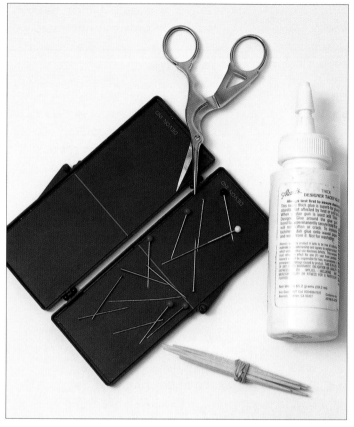

Scissors

Small sharp-pointed scissors are used for cutting intricate shapes and trimming excess paper. Scissors are also used to cut fringes if you don't use a fringing tool.

Measuring & Tracing Tools

Tracing paper – to trace copies of your pattern
• Ruler
• Protractor
• Graph Paper
• Compass

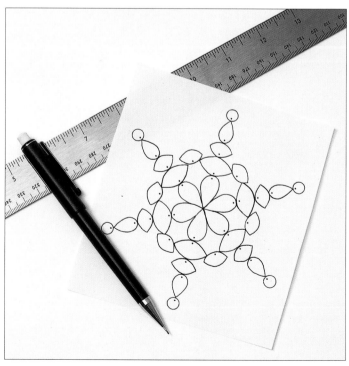

QUILLING BOARD

It takes just a few minutes to make a quilling board. Use a piece of corrugated cardboard with one smooth side, or a piece of foam core board. Cut the board larger than the pattern you plan to quill. A 9" x 12" board works for most patterns, but smaller boards are sometimes more convenient. Cover the smooth surface with a sheet of white paper. Wrap a piece of wax paper over the white sheet. When you are ready to start quilling, slip a traced copy of your pattern between the white paper and the wax paper. It will be clearly visible. You can assemble and glue the individual quilled shapes right onto the wax paper. If you are not working with a pattern, it is handy to slip a piece of tracing paper under the plastic. This will help you keep shapes even.

There is also a quality board on the market called a "Quilling Workboard." It has a clear plastic cover under which you can slip your quilling pattern. It is made of high-quality composition cork which is more self-healing than other surfaces. Pin holes will almost disappear, leaving the surface smooth.

Quilling Designer/Board

The designer/board is a multi-functional tool which is inexpensive and well worth buying. On one side are a series of circular molds in six different sizes. Allowing rolls to open in these molds makes perfectly uniform rolls. It is especially helpful for making eccentric off-center shapes that are of uniform size. There is a triangular cork area for holding your straight pins. In addition, the reverse side is cork and useful as a quilling board.

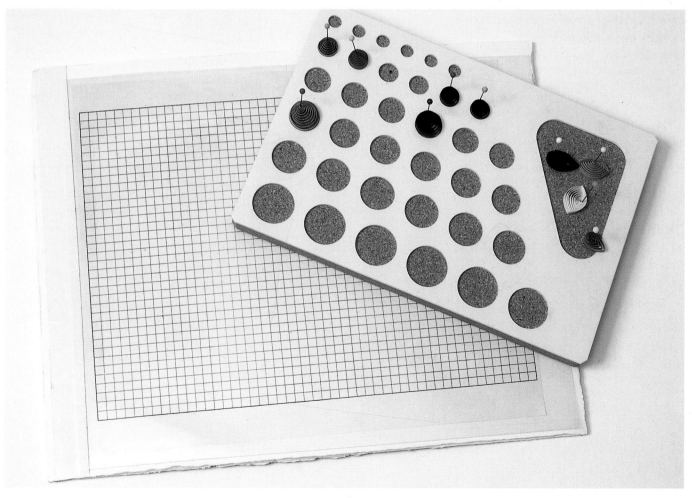

How to Quill
Using a Needle Tool

The instructions below use the example of a tight circle. This is the simplest standard shape. It is often used to make a flower center or a bud. In addition, most other shapes start with the tight circle. Be sure to wash your hands. Oil or dirt on your fingertips may discolor your paper shapes.

Tear off a strip of paper to the length needed (if following project instructions, the length will be specified). Be sure to tear the strip rather than cutting it, as the torn end will glue down much more smoothly than a cut end. Slightly moisten one end of strip and place that end against your index finger. Position the needle tool (or a hat pin) on the end of the paper. Use your thumb to press the paper around the tool. Roll the paper around the tool. Do not turn the tool as you roll the paper. Keep edges as even as possible. When finished, slip the needle from the roll's center, grasp the roll with your fingers to keep it from unwinding, and apply a small amount of glue to the end of the strip. Press the end in place against the side of the roll and hold until the glue adheres well.

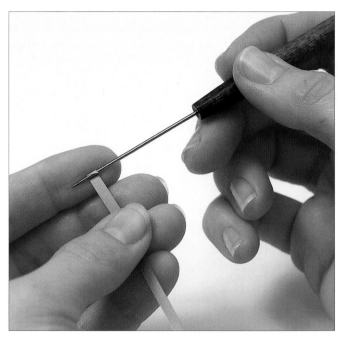

1. Position needle tool on end of paper.

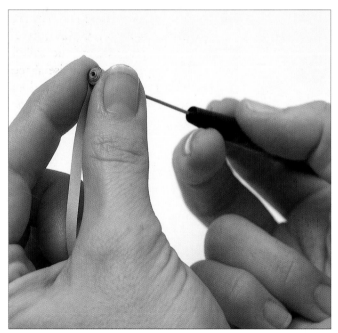

2. When finished, slip needle from roll's center.

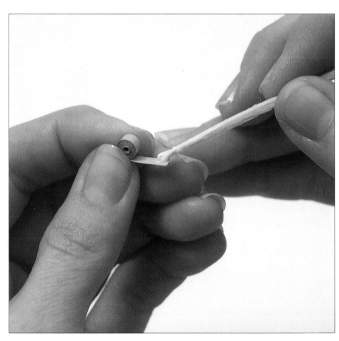

3. Glue end of strip again side of roll.

Using a Slotted Tool

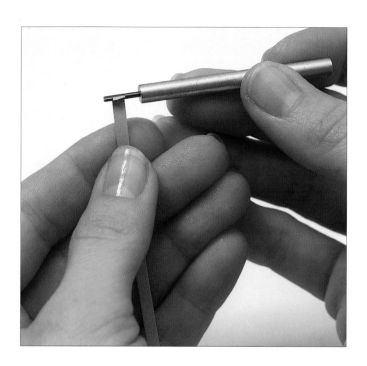

These instructions are, again, for the tight circle which is the basis or beginning of most other shapes. Thread the paper, torn to the length needed for your shape, into the slot of the tool. Adjust the slot's position to put the end of the strip just at the slot's edge, then turn the tool to roll the paper around itself. The slot will tightly grasp and hold the end of the paper. When using this quilling tool to make loose circles, it may be helpful to place a small dot of glue on the starting-end of the paper, on the side will *not* be against the tool, after inserting the paper to extend about 1/8" past the slot. This way, the center of the loose circle is glued securely, while unglued loose circles expand and lose the tight center. When finished, gently slip the tool from the roll's center and glue end of strip in place to the side of the roll.

Make Various Shapes for Your Design

Make all the different shapes your design will require. The lengths given in the instructions are the lengths of the paper strips, not the measurements of the rolled shapes. For example, a 6" marquise is a marquise shape made with a 6" long paper strip. The measurement does not refer to the finished size of the shape, which will be small.

Assembly

Glue the shapes together on your quilling board to create your design, gluing each to an adjacent shape. Use pins into the board to hold the shapes in position as you work. Use glue sparingly, only the amount needed to hold the shapes in place. Let assembled design dry.

Glue finished design onto your project.

In the finished project shown below, a quilled flower is glued onto a greeting card.

Assembly Using a Pattern

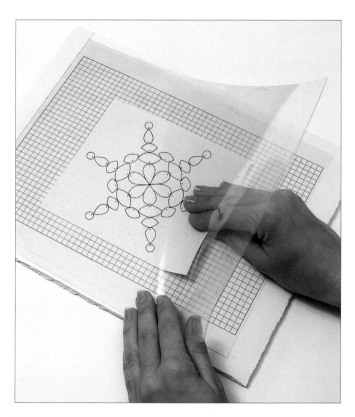

Slip your traced pattern behind the wax paper of the quilling board. It will be visible through the wax paper.

Glue the shapes for the design in place, gluing each to adjacent shapes and matching them to the pattern. Use pins into the board to hold shapes in place as you work. Leave design on the quilling board until glue dries.

The photo below shows the finished snowflake glued atop a papier mache box. See the "Christmas Quilling" section for pattern and instructions to make the snowflake design.

QUILLING SHAPES

Quilled designs are made up of individual shapes – both standard and irregular ones. Before you start your first project, practice making some of the standard shapes, using 4" lengths of 1/8" wide paper.

ROLLS

Tight Circle

The tight circle is the basis or first step of most all other shapes. Making the tight circle is described in "Using a Needle Tool" and "Using a Slotted Tool."

Loose Circle

To make a loose circle, first make a tight circle but don't glue the end. Slip it off the tool, place it on a flat surface, and let its coils expand. If outer coils stick together, turn the center coils to tighten them slightly. This will draw the outer coils in toward the center. When the circle has expanded to the size needed, glue its end in place.

When a pattern requires many loose circles the same size, the designer board is helpful. Tight circles placed into one of the molds of the board will expand to the mold's exact size. If all your circles are made with the same length of paper, they will all be the same size.

The loose circle is frequently the basis of other shapes. The circle is pinched in various ways to form the other shapes.

Teardrop

Roll and glue a loose circle. Pinch one side of the circle to a point.

Shaped Teardrop

Roll and glue a loose circle. Pinch one side to a point. Curl the point in one direction.

Marquise

Roll and glue a loose circle. Pinch it on two opposite sides.

Shaped Marquise

Make a marquise. Curl its two pinched points in opposite directions.

Crescent

Make a teardrop. Pinch a second point that is not quite opposite to the first point. Curl the two points toward each other.

Rectangle

Make a marquise. Turn it slightly and pinch again on two opposite sides.

Square or Diamond

Make a marquise. Pinch it again on two opposite sides that are opposite the first two pinched sides. The four pinched points should be equi-distant (90-degrees) from each other.

Triangle

Roll and glue a loose circle. Pinch three points at the same time, pressing the circle between your thumb and forefinger of one hand and pushing it against the side of one finger on the other hand.

Bunny Ear

Roll and glue a loose circle. Make a rounded indentation on one side. (This is similar to the crescent, but its points are closer together.)

Half Circle

Roll and glue a loose circle. Flatten one side by pinching the circle at two points.

Rolled Heart (or Arrow)

Roll and glue a loose circle. Pinch a point on one side. Make a sharp indentation on the opposite side. Be sure that all three points are very sharp.

Holly Leaf

Roll and glue a loose circle. Pinch five or six points, making a rounded indentation between each set of two points. It is helpful to use tweezers to crease the points tightly.

Grape Roll

Make a tight circle. Gently push out the center of the circle to make a conical roll. Spread a thin layer of glue on the inner surface unless this surface will be displayed. If so, apply the glue to the outer surface. Let glue dry. Grape rolls can be made with rounded, pointed, or flat ends. Grapes and berries should be just slightly rounded; for a bell, make a more pronounced point at the end. To make a flower pot, flatten the extended center before applying glue to the inner surface.

SCROLLS

Loose Scroll

Roll one end of the strip. Leave the other end loose.

Open Heart

Crease strip of paper at its center. Roll each end in toward the crease

V-Scroll

Crease strip of paper at its center. Roll each end toward the outside. To make a closed V- scroll, glue the inner surfaces of the folded section together.

S-Scroll

Roll one end of the strip toward the center. Roll the other end in the other direction toward the center to make the S-shape.

C-Scroll

Roll both ends of the strip toward the center.

Double Scroll

Tear two lengths of paper, one shorter than the other. Place the two stripes with one on top of the other, placing one end of the shorter length 1/4" from the end of the longer length. Glue strips together at the overlapping point. Roll the double strip, starting at the end that has the longer strip on the outside. Release the tension on the roll and pull slightly on the shorter length to separate the coiled strips. Glue ends together.

Triple Scroll

Fold a length of paper in half. Roll each end just a few turns. Roll the folded end down to meet the first two rolls.

Double Scroll with Flag

Fold a length of paper in half. Roll the folded strip, starting from the two loose ends. The inside strip will form a flag or loop near the crease.

ECCENTRIC SHAPES

Eccentric shapes have centers that have been pulled to one side. For instance, the center of a typical loose circle remains in the middle, but the center of an eccentric circle is pulled toward one edge of the circle with a pin and glued in place.

Eccentric Loose Circle

All eccentric shapes are made with an eccentric loose circle.

Roll a tight circle and place it in a mold on the designer quilling board. When the circle has expanded, glue its end in place. Insert a straight pin in its center and move the center to the mold's edge. Push the pin into the board to keep the center in this position. Place a small bit of glue on top of the circle between the pin and the mold's edge. Rub the glue in well so that it will spread between the coiled layers. Let glue dry before removing the pin.

When displaying the eccentric shapes, turn them upside down so the glue used in making them with not be visible.

Eccentric Teardrop

Make an eccentric loose circle. Hold the glued section between your thumb and forefinger. With your other thumb and forefinger, pinch the opposite side to a point. (The more coils you include when you pinch the shape, the sharper the point will be.)

Eccentric Marquise

Make an eccentric loose circle. Pinch two opposite sides of the circle to a point. (Be sure the glued portion is between these two points.) The more coils you pinch, the more slender your marquise will be.

Eccentric Crescent

Make an eccentric loose circle. Pinch the circle at two points that are not exactly opposite each other. Curl ends toward each other. Apply glue across the shape's center and hold until glue dries.

Eccentric Bunny Ear

Make an eccentric loose circle. Indent one side of the circle, then pinch two sharp points.

Eccentric Fan

Make an eccentric marquise. Hold each point and press in on the same side of each point, expanding the coils on each side of the marquise. Glue to hold.

SPECIAL EFFECTS
USING A FRINGING TOOL

While quilling strips can be fringed by hand with scissors, that is a tedious job and the cuts will not be as uniform as with the fringing tool. The fringing tool fringes the strips easily and quickly and creates perfectly uniform cuts. The tool is adjustable for use with 1/4" and 3/8" paper widths.

HOW TO MAKE A FRINGED FLOWER

1. Fringe along one side of the paper strip with either scissors or a fringing tool. If you use scissors, remember that the closer the cuts are to each other, the more attractive the flower will be. If you wish to make a fringed flower without a center, proceed to step 2. If you wish to make a fringed flower with center, glue a narrower strip to the fringed wider strip, gluing them end to end as shown in *photo 1*.

2. Roll fringed paper into a tight circle. If making a fringed flower with center, begin coiling with narrower strip of unfringed paper. See *photo 2*.

3. Glue the end closed as shown in *photo 3*. Spread the fringes with your fingernail so that they open up from the roll's center. Curl the outermost ring of fringes with the needle tool.

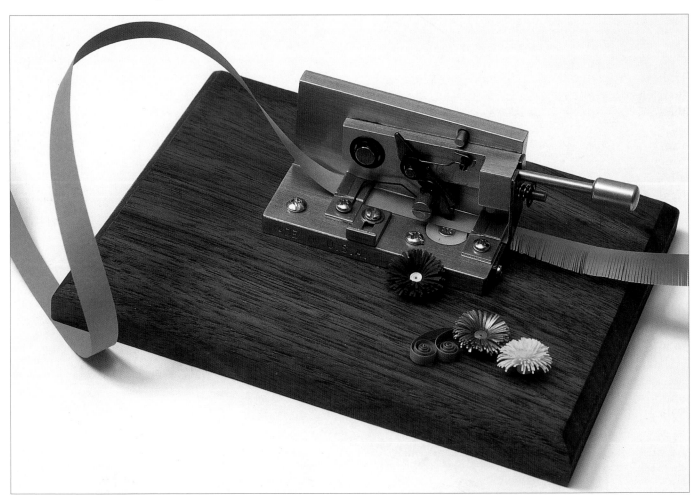

Photo 1   *Photo 2*   *Photo 3*

Two-Tone Fringed Flower

Fringe a length of two different colors of paper. Place the strips together, one on top of the other (with fringed sides on the same side), and treat as one. Roll them into a single tight circle and glue closed. Spread fringed edges with your fingernail.

Finished Example: the metallic gold flower fringed flowers are examples of the fringed flowers with centers. The burgundy flowers are examples of fringed flowers without centers. For complete instructions on making the gift cards shown, see "Great Greeting Cards & Gift Tags" chapter.

How to Make a Spiral

Place one end of the paper length at an angle on the quilling tool. Roll the strip down the tool to make a spiral, keeping a little tension on it with the thumb and forefinger of your hand holding the tool. When you reach the base of the tool, let the starting end of the spiral slip off the tool while you continue to roll. This creates a tightly-rolled regular spiral.

To make a loose spiral, first roll a tight one. Remove it from the tool. Run the side of the needle down the inside of the paper length from the loose end toward the tight end (like curling a piece of ribbon with a blade of scissors). Stop just before the spiral's tight end so you won't remove all the tension from its point.

V-shaped double spirals are made by rolling from each end of the paper strip. ∽

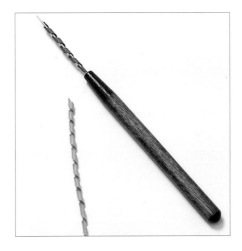

PROJECTS

Whatever category you like best, whatever type of item you need for a unique touch or a special gift, you're sure to find in this collection. Quilled projects include photo mats and framed designs, greeting cards and gift tags, jewelry, home decor accessories, projects for special occasions such as showers and for particular seasons, and, of course, projects for Christmas. Some designs are simple and quick, others are intricate and worth the time. Start a project today for quilling fun in one of these categories:

Photo Mats & Framed Designs

Great Greeting Cards & Gift Tags

Unique Quilled Jewelry

Quilled Home Decor Accessories

Quilled Projects For Special Occasions

Christmas Quilling

PHOTO MATS & FRAMED DESIGNS

Mats are "a natural" for quilled designs. They look terrific with this extra touch surrounding a photo or keepsake such as a wedding invitation. The projects here even include an easy frame made of corrugated cardboard. From Victorian to modern, there's a variety of styles and projects to make your framed items special.

The kiss of the sun for pardon,
the song of the birds for mirth.
One is nearer God's heart in a garden
than anywhere else on earth.

Dorothy Gurney

Sunflower Garden Pattern

Photo & Instructions on pages 26 & 27

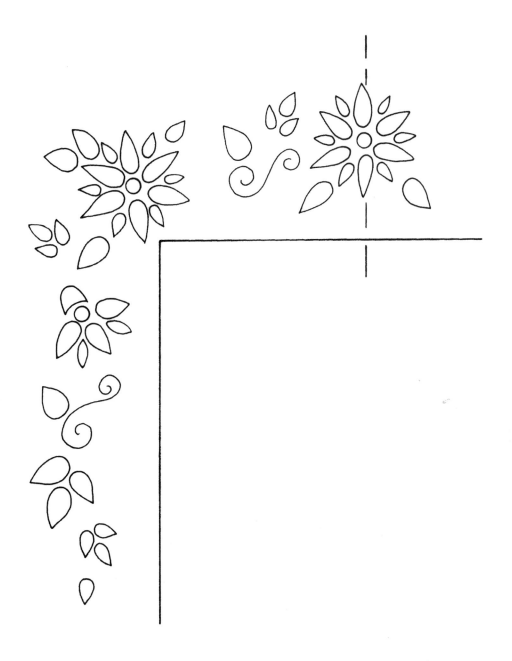

Reverse pattern for second side.

SUNFLOWER GARDEN

Designed by Patty Cox

This sunny mat was used to frame a poem that begins "The kiss of the sun..."
It is framed with woodtones to complete the natural theme. This mat would
also look great framing a photo of the sunflower in your life.

MATERIALS

Quilling Paper, 1/8" wide:
Dark Brown
Dark Green
Yellow Gold

Other Supplies:
Quilling tool
8" x 10" tan mat
Clear drying craft glue

Pattern on page 25

INSTRUCTIONS

Large Sunflowers (Make 3):
1. Roll a 5" brown **tight circle** for each flower center (3 total).
2. Make six 5" yellow **eccentric teardrops** for each large sunflower (18 total). These are larger petals.
3. Make six 2-1/2" yellow **teardrops** for each large sunflower. Pinch each into a teardrop for smaller petals. (18 total)
4. Glue petals around center according to pattern.

Small Sunflowers (Make 2):
1. Roll a 5" brown **tight circle** for each flower center (2 total).
2. Make three 5" yellow **eccentric teardrops** for each small sunflower (6 total). These are larger petals.
3. Make two 2-1/2" yellow **teardrops** for each small sunflower (4 total). These are smaller petals.
4. Make a 5" dark green **bunny ear** for each small sunflower calyx.
5. Glue petals around center according to pattern. Glue a calyx to each small sunflower.

Sunflower Buds (Make 2 large and 6 small):
1. Make a 5" yellow **eccentric teardrop** for each large sunflower bud.
2. Make a 2-1/2" yellow **teardrop** for each small sunflower buds.

Leaves (Make 16 large, 16 small):
1. Make a 5" dark green **teardrop** for each large leaf (16 total).
2. Make a 2-1/2"dark green **teardrop** for each small leaf (16 total).
3. Roll four 5" dark green **S-scrolls.**

Assembly:
1. Glue two leaves to base of each bud – large leaves to large buds, small leaves to small buds.
2. Position and glue scrolls, sunflowers, buds with leaves, and remaining leaves on mat board according to pattern. (Reverse pattern for second side when tracing.) ∾

The kiss of the sun for pardon,

the song of the birds for mirth.

One is nearer God's heart in a garden

than anywhere else on earth.

Dorothy Gurney

SPRING GARDEN PHOTO MAT

Designed by Patty Cox

What more beautiful way to frame a dried pansy displayed on handmade papers? The spirit comes alive at the sight of the lovely spring colors. And filigree metal frame chosen here is reminiscent of a garden gate.

MATERIALS

Quilling Paper, 1/8" wide, 5" lengths:
Dark pink
Pink
Pale Yellow
Lime Green

Other Supplies:
Quilling tool
8" x 10" black mat
Clear drying craft glue

Pattern on page 30

INSTRUCTIONS

Large Pink Flowers (Make 3: 2 Pink, 1 Dark Pink):
1. Roll a pale yellow **tight circle** for each flower center (3 total).
2. Make ten pink and five dark pink **teardrops** for petals.
3. Glue five dark pink petals around one flower center and five pink petals around each remaining flower center.

Small Pink Flowers (Make 5: 1 Pink, 4 Dark Pink):
1. Make one pink **marquise**. Make four dark pink **marquises**. These are center petals.
2. Make two pink **shaped teardrops**. Make eight dark pink **shaped teardrops**. These are side petals.
3. Make a lime green **bunny ear** for each calyx (5 total).
4. Glue a marquise on center top of each bunny ear. Glue a matching color shaped teardrop, pointing outward, on each side of each marquise.

Flower Buds (Make 4: 1 Pink and 3 Dark Pink):
1. Make three dark pink and one light pink **teardrops** for buds.
2. Make a lime green **bunny ear** for each calyx (4 total).
3. Glue a calyx to bottom of each bud.

Scrolled Vines (Make 9):
Make nine lime green **S-scrolls**.

Leaves (Make 10):
Make ten lime green **teardrops**.

Assembly:
Arrange and glue flowers, vines, and leaves and mat according to pattern. ∽

Spring Garden Photo Mat Pattern

Instructions & Photo on pages 28 & 29

Frilly Oval Photo Mat Pattern

Instructions & Photo on pages 32 & 33

FRILLY OVAL PHOTO MAT

Designed by Patty Cox

The look of lace surrounds a special photo with the quilling on this oval mat.

MATERIALS

Quilling Paper, 1/8" wide, 5" lengths:
White
Off-white

Other Supplies:
Quilling tool
Frame and burgundy mat with oval opening, 5" x 7"
Eight silver seed beads
Clear drying craft glue

Pattern on page 31

INSTRUCTIONS

Fan Shaped Huskings (Make 24 total):
1. Make eighteen white **3-point fan shaped huskings.** (Use pins 1, 2, 5, and 6.)
2. Make four off-white **3-point fan shaped huskings.** (Use pins 1, 2, 3 and 4.)
3. Make two **4-point fan shaped huskings.** (Omit pin 2. Use pins 1, 3, 4, 5, and 6.)

Roll Quilled Shapes (Make 38 total):
1. Roll eighteen off-white **tight circles.**
2. Roll eight white **eccentric loose circles.**
3. Roll twelve off-white **eccentric loose circles.**

Assembly:
1. Glue scrolls and coiled shapes together according to pattern.
2. Glue design to mat around oval opening.
3. Arrange and glue silver seed beads on mat as shown in photo of project. ∞

HOW TO MAKE HUSKINGS

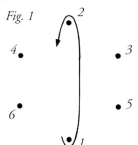

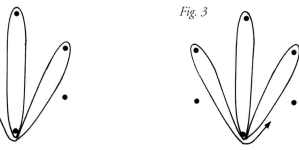

These shapes are made by winding the paper around a series of pins. Straight and fan-shaped huskings are the most often used huskings, but there's no limit to the different shapes and sizes huskings can be by simply varying the positions of your pins.

Fan-Shaped Huskings: The pins are positioned differently for fan-shaped huskings, but the procedure is similar. Place pins as shown in Fig. 1. For added stability, wind around Pins 1 and 2 twice. Also glue the paper periodically. Fan-shaped huskings can be made with or without a "collar." To make a collar, wind several loops around the exterior of the shape before gluing the end of the strip in place. Add a dot of glue at the Pin 1 position before removing the pins. (To make several huskings of uniform size, replace all the pins in the same holes.

ROSEBUDS & BABY FRAMED ANNOUNCEMENT

Designed by Patty Cox

*Pink and sweet – the baby and the rosebuds. This is a wonderful decoration
for a baby announcement. It is framed in a soft pink oval frame.*

MATERIALS

Quilling Paper, 1/8" wide:
Pink
Soft green

Other Supplies:
Quilling tool
Baby announcement cut to an oval,
    approx. 4-1/4" x 6"
Pink oval frame to fit announcement
18 small 3mm or 4mm pearls
Multi-purpose bond cement
Tweezers

INSTRUCTIONS

Rosebuds (Make 10 Large & 14 Small):
1. Make a 5" pink **teardrop** for each large rosebud.
2. Make a 2-1/2" pink **teardrop** for each small rosebud.

Leaves (Make 26):
Make a 2-1/2" soft green **teardrop** for each leaf.

Calyxes (Make 8):
Make a 2-1/2" soft green **bunny ear** for each calyx.

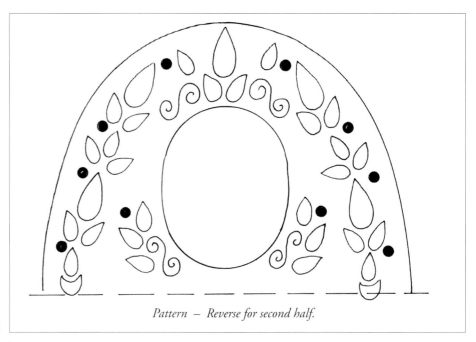

Pattern – Reverse for second half.

Vines (Make 4):
Make a 2-1/2" soft green **S-scroll** for each vine.

Assembly:
1. Glue two leaves under each large rosebud.
2. Glue a calyx under eight of the small rosebuds.
3. Glue rosebuds, leaves, and scrolls in position on announcement according to pattern.
4. Hold pearls with tweezers. Dip in bond cement. Position between rosebuds as shown in photo of project. ∾

Kate Elena Reilly

born on this day
September 22, 1998
to Paula & William Reilly

weighing
5 lb. 13 oz.

VICTORIAN REMEMBRANCE

Designed by Patty Cox

The curls and turns of a quilled border fit in perfectly with the frills of the Victorian era. This framed print of a Victorian shoe is a good example. Find a similar Victorian print to place in your frame or use the mat to enhance a photo.

MATERIALS

Quilling Paper, 1/8" wide, 5" lengths:
Pink

Other Supplies:
Quilling tool
Ivory 6" x 6" mat with 3-1/2" round mat opening
Sixteen 3/16" white pearls
Eight gold seed beads
Clear drying craft glue
6" x 6" gold frame

INSTRUCTIONS

Open Hearts (Make 4):
Make four pink **open hearts.**

Tight Circles (Make 8):
Roll eight pink **tight circles.**

V-Scrolls (Make 8):
Make eight pink **V-scrolls.**

Marquises (Make 20):
Make twenty pink **marquises.**

Loose Circles (Make 20):
Roll twenty pink **loose circles.**

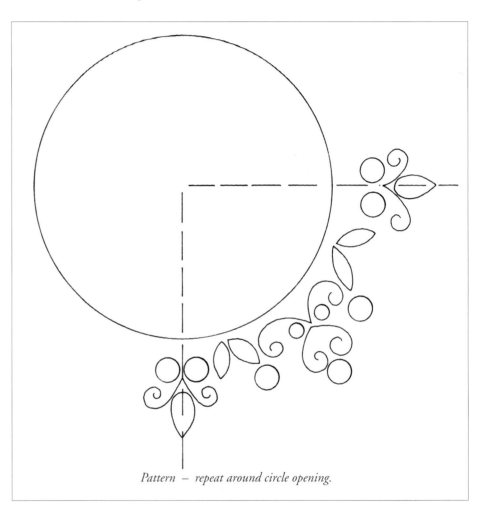

Pattern — repeat around circle opening.

Assembly:
1. Glue scrolls and coiled shapes together according to pattern. (When tracing pattern, reverse pattern for top, then reverse pattern for left side.)
2. Glue design around the 3-1/2" opening in mat.
3. Glue gold seed beads in centers of tight circles.
4. Glue pearls between scrolls and marquises as shown in photo of project. ❧

Wedding Keepsake Pattern

Instructions & Photo on pages 40 & 41

Upper Left Corner

Bottom right corner

WEDDING KEEPSAKE

Designed by Kathi Malarchuk Bailey

Peach roses and white petal flowers with pearls are reminiscent of a bride's bouquet as it decorates this framed wedding invitation.

MATERIALS

Quilling Paper:
1/8" Wide
Green
Pale Peach
White
3/8" Wide
Pale Peach

Other Supplies:
Quilling tool (slotted tool recommended for the roses)
Wedding invitation
Off-white crackled finish precut mat, 11" x 14" with 7-1/2" x 9-1/2" rectangular opening
Off-white crackled finish precut mat, 8" x 10" with 3-1/2" x 6-1/2" rectangular opening
Gold shadowbox frame, 11" x 14"
Clear drying craft glue
Cardboard, 1/2" thick

Pattern on pages 38, 39

INSTRUCTIONS

Roses (Make 10):
1. Tear ten 1/2" lengths of 3/8" pale peach paper. Tear one 3" length of 1/8" pale peach paper for each rose.
2. Using the side of the needle quilling tool, curl the two corners of one end of each 1/2" length. Curl petals back. On other end of paper piece, cut a tiny slit. Overlap paper at the slit and glue together. This forms a cupped and rolled petal. Make ten petals.
3. To assemble rose, glue five petals together in a circle. This will be the front set of petals. Glue the other five petals behind these front petals.
4. Role the 3" length of 1/8" paper into a loose circle. Glue this loose circle into center of rose.

White Teardrop Flowers (Make 8):
1. Cut three 1-1/2" lengths of 1/8" pale peach paper for each flower and roll a **tight circle** with each (24 total). Three tight circles makes each flower center.
2. Make five 5" white **shaped teardrops** for each flower (40 petals total).
3. Glue five shaped teardrops together with points at center for each flower. Glue three tight circles on top at center of each flower. Glue three small pearls around outside of each flower center.

Leaves (Make 26 Large & 17 Small):
1. Make a 6" green **marquise** for each large leaf.
2. Make a 3" green **marquise** for each small leaf.

Rosebuds (Make 6):
Make a 3" **teardrop** of 1/8" pale peach paper for each rosebud.

White Flower Buds (Make 12):
Roll a 3" **loose circle** for each bud.

Vines (Make 4 large and 18 small):
1. Make a 6" green loose **S-scroll** for each large vine.
2. Make a 1-1/2" green loose **scroll** for each small vine.

Assembly:
1. Mount the wedding invitation in inner and outer mats. Cut four 2" strips of 1/2"-thick cardboard for spacers between the two mats (to hold the outer mat forward for more dimension). Glue these to the four outside corners of the bottom (inner) mat.
2. Glue quilled flowers, buds, leaves, and vines on outer and inner mats according to pattern.
3. Place in shadowbox frame. ∽

Mr. and Mrs. Ralph Edward Harwell
request the honour of your presence
at the marriage of their daughter
Amy Dawn
to
Battle Alexander Beasley
son of Dr. and Mrs. William Boodie Rogers Beasley
on Saturday, the twenty-seventh of September
nineteen hundred and ninety-seven
at two o'clock in the afternoon
All Saints Chapel
Sewanee, Tennessee

Reception immediately following
at Brinkwood

STRIKING GRAPHICS FRAME

Designed by Holly Witt

Quilling goes modern with this bold black and white design on cardboard frame. Complete it by placing it in a black frame.

MATERIALS

Quilling Paper, 1/8" wide:
Black
White

Other Supplies:
Quilling tool
Corrugated cardboard frame with smooth surfaces, 9" square x 1/2" thick with 3" square opening
Clear drying craft glue

INSTRUCTIONS

Squares (Make 44 – 22 black, 22 white):
1. Make 22 black 5" **squares.**
2. Make 22 white 5" **squares.**

Diamonds (Make 16):
1. Make four black **triangles** for each diamond (64 total).
2. Arrange triangles with flat side toward inside of diamond, points touching adjacent triangle, to make diamond shapes. Glue points where they touch points of adjacent triangles.
3. Roll 3" white **tight circles.** Make 48. These will be glued to the points of the diamonds. However, wait until gluing the diamonds to the frame because you won't need a circle glued to every point.

Assembly:
1. Glue squares around edge of opening, alternating black and white.

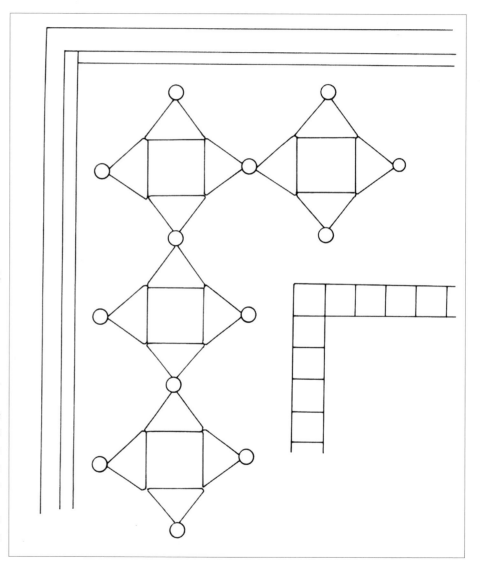

2. Glue diamonds with a white tight circle at each point around outside of frame, according to pattern. (Adjacent diamonds will share one tight circle at their adjacent points.)
3. Glue a strip of black paper around each side of the frame, approximately 1/4" in from edge.
4. Place in black frame. ∞

GREAT GREETING CARDS & GIFT TAGS

Greeting cards or gift tags and quilled designs look like they were made for each other. After all, they are paper on paper but, oh, in what a gorgeous way! When you want a birthday or anniversary or "thank you" greeting or gift to be special, consider making one of the projects here.

A friend
hears the song
in your heart,
and sings it
back to you
when you've
forgotten.

May All
of Your Dreams
Come True

BUTTERFLY GIFT CARD

Designed by Patty Cox

The quilled decorations on this gift card are the gift – not just because they are lovely, but because they are jewelry! That's right, quilled earrings and a stickpin create the card's decorations.

MATERIALS

Quilled Butterfly Earrings & Stickpin (instructions in the "Unique Quilled Jewelry" section)

Purple corrugated paper, 10" x 8-1/2"

Metallic turquoise paper, enough to cut a 2-3/4" x 4-1/4" oval and a 2" x 1-1/2" rectangle

White paper, 9" x 7-1/2" sheet and 1-1/2" x 1-1/4" piece

Black permanent pen

Pinking shears

White organza ribbon

Clear drying craft glue

Tapestry needle

INSTRUCTIONS

1. Fold the purple corrugated paper in half (to 5" x 8-1/2").
2. Using pattern, cut oval opening in front of card (refer to photo of project).
3. Write the message (pattern given) on white paper. Tear paper into a 1-1/2" x 1-1/4" rectangle. Glue this rectangle on metallic turquoise paper. Tear edges of metallic paper 3/16" larger all around than message paper. Glue message on card front as shown in photo.
4. With pinking shears, cut on oval from metallic turquoise paper 1/4" larger all around than opening on card. Cut out oval from center of this that is the same size as oval on card (use pattern). Glue this metal-

May All of Your Dreams Come True

lic turquoise border around oval opening on card. Let glue dry.

5. Fold 9" x 7-1/2" paper in half (to 4-1/2" x 7-1/2"). Place in center of folded corrugated card.
6. With a tapestry needle, whip stitch closed edge (left edge) of card with organza ribbon, securing all layers of paper. Tie a bow with remaining ribbon and tie to upper left corner of card.
7. Secure stickpin on white inside paper so that it shows through oval opening of card. Stick earring backs through corrugated paper front of card and secure. ∞

May All
of Your Dreams
Come True

FLORAL GREETING

Designed by Patty Cox

So lovely, so much dimension and texture, and it's all paper! The handmade papers and corrugated paper make a perfect backdrop for the colorful quilled floral design on this card.

MATERIALS

Quilling Paper, 1/8" wide, 5" lengths:
Green
Lavender
Pale Yellow
Pink
Purple
Soft Green

Other Supplies:
Quilling tool
Off-white card stock, 10" x 7" folded in half (to 5" x 7")
Purple handmade paper, 4" x 6"
Ecru handmade paper, 4" x 6"
Corrugated cardboard with one rippled side, 3" x 5"
Clear drying craft glue

INSTRUCTIONS

Pink Flowers (Make 3):
1. Roll pale yellow **tight circles** for each flower center (3 total).
2. Make six pink **teardrops** per flower (18 total), for petals.
3. Glue six petals around each flower center.

Yellow Lilies (Make 10):
1. Cut ten pieces of paper to varying lengths from 2" to 5".
2. With each length, make a **shaped teardrop**.

Purple Hyacinths (Make 2):
1. Roll ten lavender **tight circles**.
2. Roll seven purple **tight circles**.
3. Roll seven lavender **loose circles**.
4. Roll five purple **loose circles**.
5. When assembling, arrange and glue circles together according to pattern to make two hyacinth clusters.

Leaves (Make 12: 4 green, 8 soft green):
1. Make four green **teardrops**.
2. Make eight soft green **teardrops**.

Assembly:
1. Fold cardstock in half, making a 5" x 7" card.
2. Tear edges of purple handmade paper. Tear ecru handmade paper 1/4" smaller all around than purple paper. Glue handmade papers in center of card front, centering ecru paper on purple paper. Center and glue corrugated cardboard on ecru paper.
3. Arrange and glue flowers, leaves, and stems on corrugated cardboard according to pattern. Start with a 4" soft green length of quilling paper for one lily stem and a 2" length for second lily stem on corrugated paper. Glue seven lilies on the 4" stem, graduating from smallest at top to largest at bottom; glue three lilies on the 2" stem. Arrange other flowers and leaves as shown. ∞

AUTUMN GREETINGS

Designed by Patty Cox

Quilled autumn maple leaves in many colors drift down the side of this cor-rugated card while the cinnamon stick spine adds a delightful fragrance.

MATERIALS

Quilling Paper, 1/8" wide:
Brown
Orange
Red
Yellow Gold

Other Supplies:
Quilling tool
Tan corrugated cardboard with one rippled side, 10-1/2" x 8-1/2"
Ivory handmade paper, 11" x 8-1/2"
Twenty metallic gold seed beads
Gold metallic wax
Two cinnamon sticks, 8-1/2" long
Natural raffia
Clear drying craft glue
Paper punch
Craft knife

A friend
hears the song
in your heart,
and sings it
back to you
when you've
forgotten.

INSTRUCTIONS

Maple Leaves (Make 5):
1. Make two yellow gold leaves and one each of orange, red, and brown.
2. For each leaf, make a 6" **teardrop** for top (smallest) point.
3. For middle (medium) leaf points of each leaf, make two 7" **teardrops.**
4. For bottom (largest) leaf points of each leaf, make two 10" **teardrops.**
5. For each leaf, make a 6" long **triangle.** (This is like a **shaped teardrop** with the rounded end flattened.)
6. Glue the two bottom points together, round end to round end. Glue the two medium points together, round end to round end,

and glue these to bottom points. Glue round end of top point to top of leaf. Glue the point of the triangle between bottom points for stem. (See pattern.)

Assembly:
1. Fold front of corrugated cardboard to be 5" wide, with the back of card extending beyond right edge of front.
2. With a craft knife, cut out an oval opening according to pattern centered on front of card.
3. Edge the oval and the right edge of card front with gold metallic wax.
4. Fold ivory paper in half and place inside card. The open edge will extend beyond the front of card but not the back of card. Edge the ivory paper with gold metallic wax.
5. Mark position of message. Write or print the message on the paper inside so that it shows through the oval in the card.
6. Punch holes down left side of card, making sure they go through the folded paper inside as well. Place cinnamon sticks along the left edge. With raffia, wrap around left edge of card and cinnamon sticks with a "whip stitch" through the holes. Tie raffia ends in a bow at upper left corner of card.
7. Glue quilled maple leaves on card as shown in photo of project. Glue gold seed beads in a scattered pattern between and around leaves. ∽

A friend
hears the song
in your heart,
and sings it
back to you
when you've
forgotten.

BIRD OF PARADISE GIFT TAG

Designed by Patty Cox

An exotic quilled bird of paradise on folded paper makes a unique and beautiful gift tag.

MATERIALS

Quilling Paper, 1/8" wide, 10" lengths:
Orange
Purple
Dark green

Other Supplies:
Quilling tool
Ivory handmade paper, 3-1/4" x 5-1/4"
Lavender paper, 3-5/8" x 6"
Light olive paper, 4-1/8" x 6-1/2"
White organza ribbon, 18" length
Gold metallic ribbon, 18" length
Clear drying craft glue
Glue stick
Gold metallic wax
Paper punch

INSTRUCTIONS

Bird of Paradise:
1. Make three 10" orange **teardrops** for flower top.
2. Make one 10" purple **teardrop** for lower part of flower.
3. Make a 5" dark green **S-scroll** for stem.
4. Make two 10" **teardrops** for leaves.

Assembly:
1. Tear edges of ivory handmade paper, lavender paper, and light olive paper.
2. Rub edge of lavender paper with gold metallic wax.
3. Center and glue papers on top of one another, largest on bottom, smallest on top. Let dry.
4. Fold papers in half.
5. Punch a hole in top left of tag.
6. Glue bird of paradise quilled design on front of tag according to pattern.
7. Tie gold and white ribbons in a bow through the hole. ∾

GOLDEN GARDEN CARDS & TAGS

Designed by Malinda Johnston

What a nice touch for someone to receive a gift card or tag with dimension, texture, and beauty – especially when it's hand quilled by you.

Golden Garden Notecard

MATERIALS

Quilling Paper:
1/8" wide
Deep Aqua
Ivory
Metallic gold (quill trim)
Soft Green
3/8" wide
Metallic gold (quill trim)

Other Supplies:
Quilling tool
Fringing tool
Ivory gift card with gold trim,
   approx. 3" x 3-3/4"
Metallic gold paper
Clear drying craft glue

INSTRUCTIONS

Petal Flowers (Make 3):
1. Roll a 3" soft green **tight circle** for each flower center (3 total).
2. Make five 3" ivory **teardrops** for each flower (15 total). These are petals.
3. Make five 3" soft green **loose scrolls.**
4. Glue round ends of five teardrops around each tight circle.
5. Glue two scrolls to two flowers, and one scroll to the third flower.

Butterfly body pattern

Butterfly

Petal Flower

Fringed Flower

Fringed Flowers (Make 5):
Make **fringed flowers with center**, using a 3" length of 1/8" deep aqua and a 3" length of 3/8" metallic gold quill trim for each.

Butterfly (Make 1):
1. BODY: Using the pattern, cut a butterfly body piece from a sheet of metallic gold paper. Roll on needle tool, beginning at the wide end of the triangle. Glue the end.
2. WINGS (make 2): For each wing, make a 6" and a 4" ivory **eccentric teardrop.** Wrap a length of 1/8" gold quill trim around each teardrop and glue.
3. Glue a small and a large teardrop together for each wing as shown on pattern. Glue wings at an angle to sides of body so that wings are elevated forward.

Assembly:
Position and glue the flowers and butterfly on front of notecard as shown in photo of project. ∞

Flowery Note Card

MATERIALS

Quilling Paper:
1/8" wide
Green
Raspberry
White
3/8" wide
Raspberry

Other Supplies:
Quilling tool
Fringing tool
Ivory V-flap notecard with gold trim,
   5" x 3-1/4"
Clear drying craft glue

INSTRUCTIONS

Petal Flower (Make 1):
1. Make five 5" **teardrops** from 1/8" raspberry paper. Glue round ends together in a circle.

Continued on page 56

Pictured on page 55

Flowery Note Card (cont.)

2. Roll a 4" white **tight circle** for flower center and glue in center on top of petals.

Loop Leaves (Make 2):

1. With a 4-3/4" length of green paper for each, make a 5-loop **fan husking**. If needed, mark the length of paper as shown in Fig. 1 to show length of each loop.
2. Glue a leaf on each side of the petal flower.

Fringed Flowers (Make 5):

Roll a 4" length of 3/8" fringed raspberry paper for each **fringed flower.**

Marquise Leaves (Make 6):

Make a 5" green **marquise** for each leaf.

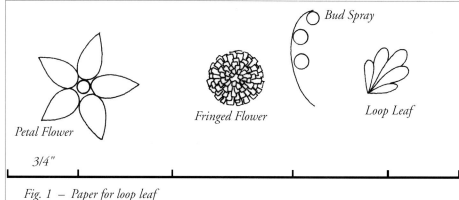

Fig. 1 – Paper for loop leaf

Bud Spray (Make 2):

1. Roll three raspberry **tight circles** for each spray, using 1", 2", and 3" lengths of paper.
2. Glue three sizes of tight circles to a short, curved length of green paper, with the smallest circle at the end, for each spray.

Assembly:

1. Glue the petal flower and three fringed flowers to the center of the V-flap.
2. Position a fringed flower, three marquise leaves, and a bud spray in each lower corner and glue in place. ∽

Bells & Bow Gift Tag

MATERIALS

Quilling Paper:

Metallic gold (quill trim), 1/8" and 3/8" wide

Ivory, 1/4" wide

Other Supplies:

Quilling tool

Ivory fold-over card, 3" x 3"

Clear drying craft glue

INSTRUCTIONS

Bell (Make 2):

1. Glue two 24" lengths of 1/8" metallic gold quill trim together end to end for each bell.
2. Roll this 48" length of gold metallic paper into a **grape roll** for each bell.
3. Roll a 3" **tight circle** using 1/8" metallic gold quill trim for each clapper. Cut a narrow piece of gold quill trim and glue to the tight circle. Glue this into each bell as a

4. Roll a 3" gold **tight circle** and glue to top of each bell.

Ribbon:

1. Make a 3" length of ribbon and two short streamers by gluing 1/4" wide ivory paper lengthwise to the center of 3/8" wide gold quill trim. Glue a length of 1/8" wide gold quill trim lengthwise to the center of the 1/4" ivory paper.
2. Make the bow with a 5" length of this same combination of three papers. First glue the ends of the 3/8" wide paper around onto its center. (Curving the wider paper before adding the other strips will make a smoother bow.) Next glue the ivory paper to the wider gold paper, then the narrow gold paper to the ivory paper. Add a shorter length of the same three papers around center of bow.

Assembly:

Arrange and glue the ribbon and bells on the front of notecard as shown in the photo of project. ∽

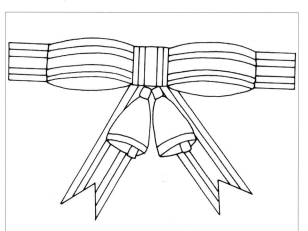

OPEN HEART GIFT RIBBON

Designed by Betty Cristy

Now who but you would add special decorations to the ribbon on a gift?
The recipient will be taken with your extra effort and sense of beauty.

MATERIALS

Quilling Paper, 1/8" wide:
White

Other Supplies:
Quilling tool
Green ribbon, 1-1/4" wide
Clear drying craft glue

INSTRUCTIONS

Make open hearts and glue them evenly spaced, on ribbon on front of gift-package after wrapping package.

UNIQUE QUILLED JEWELRY

Quilled butterflies or bees, posies, or art deco shapes all make great jewelry. In the projects here, there are a stickpin and earrings set, a pendant, and fashion pins – even one especially for Christmas holiday wear. These make wonderful gift items as well as fashion accessories for yourself.

BUTTERFLY EARRINGS & STICKPIN

Designed by Patty Cox

Pretty on the ears, pretty on the lapel, and pretty when used as the decorations on a gift card. (See the "Butterfly Gift Card" in the "Great Greeting Cards & Gift Tags" section.)

MATERIALS

Quilling Paper, 1/8" wide:
Lavender
Light Turquoise
Purple
Turquoise

Other Supplies:
Quilling Tool
Tweezers
Stickpin
Two earring backs
Clear drying craft glue
Flexible industrial glue
Jewelry glaze

INSTRUCTIONS

Butterfly Body, Head & Antennae:
1. BODY: Make a 5" lavender **teardrop** for each butterfly.
2. HEAD: Roll a 5" purple **tight circle** for each butterfly.
3. ANTENNAE: Roll two 2-1/2" lavender **tight circles** for each butterfly (6 total).

Butterfly Wings (6 wings – 2 per butterfly):
1. Roll four 5" purple **tight circles** per butterfly (12 total).
2. Roll two 2-1/2" lavender **tight circles** per butterfly (6 total).
3. Make two 2-1/2" turquoise **S-scrolls** per butterfly (6 total).
4. Make two 2-1/2" light turquoise **S-scrolls** per butterfly (6 total).
5. Roll two 2-1/2" light turquoise **loose circles** per butterfly (6 total).
6. Roll two 2-1/2" light turquoise **teardrops** per butterfly (6 total).

Assembly:
1. Assemble each butterfly according to the pattern. Let glue dry.
2. Using tweezers, dip each butterfly into jewelry glaze. Allow excess glaze to drip back into container. Let dry on wax paper or crumpled aluminum foil.
3. With flexible industrial glue, glue stickpin on back of one butterfly and an earring back on the back of two butterflies. ∽

PINK POSIES PIN

Designed by Patty Cox

*A little box of flowers can make the perfect fashion pin. Quill the flowers and leaves
and encase them in a clear box lid. Add a pin to the back, and you're in fashion.*

MATERIALS

**Quilling Paper, 1/8" wide, 2-1/2"
   lengths:**
Green
Pale Pink
Pale Yellow
Soft Green

Other Supplies:
Quilling tool
Clear acrylic box lid, 1" x 2"
White backing paper, 1" x 2"
Clear drying craft glue
Flexible industrial glue
Pin back

INSTRUCTIONS

**Pink Flowers (Make 14 petals & 3
centers):**
1. Roll three pale yellow **tight circles**
   for flower centers.
2. Make fourteen pale pink **teardrops**
   for petals.
3. Make four soft green **bunny ears**
   for calyxes.
4. Glue six petals around one flower center.
5. Glue three petals on each remaining flower center.
6. Glue a bunny ear below each 3-petal flower.
7. Glue a bunny ear below each remaining single petal for buds.

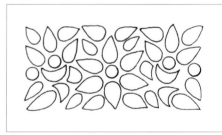

Leaves (Make 18 total):
1. Make ten soft green **teardrops**.
2. Make six green loose **teardrops**.
3. Make two green **squares**.

Assembly:
1. Arrange flowers, buds, and leaves on inside of acrylic box lid according to pattern.
2. Spread clear drying craft glue on surface of paper backing. Press glue side of
   paper backing on lid back against quilled design.
3. Glue pin back on paper backing with flexible industrial glue. ∞

HOLLY PHOTO PIN

Designed by Patty Cox

Hang a favorite little framed photo from a quilled holly sprig. Pin in to your lapel for a perfect holiday fashion touch.

MATERIALS

Quilling Paper, 1/8" wide:
Green
Red

Other Supplies:
Quilling tool
Photo frame charm, 1"
Small pin back
Jump ring
Jewelry glaze
Clear drying craft glue
Flexible industrial glue
Tweezers

INSTRUCTIONS

Holly Berries (Make 3):
Roll three 2-1/2" red **tight circles**.

Holly Leaves (Make 4):
For each leaf, make a green **holly leaf shape**.

Assembly:
1. Glue leaves and berries together according to pattern. Let dry.
2. Using tweezers, dip quilled holly sprig into jewelry glaze. Allow excess glaze to drip back into container. Let dry on wax paper or crumpled aluminum foil.
3. Place photo in charm. Crimp back edges of charm closed.
4. Secure the small pin back to top of charm with a jump ring.
5. With flexible industrial glue, glue holly sprig onto pin back. ∞

ART DECO PENDANT

Designed by Kathi Malarchuk Bailey

The art deco style of design is a combination of various shapes. This makes it perfect for quilling. The pin is a little touch of art deco excitement for a favorite dress or jacket.

MATERIALS

Quilling Paper, 1/8" wide:
Dark Purple
Silver (Quill Trim)
White

Other Supplies:
Quilling tool
Large silvertone jump ring
Silvertone chain
Clear drying craft glue

INSTRUCTIONS

1. Make eleven 6" dark purple **shaped teardrops.**
2. Make three 6" white **loose circles.**
3. Make twelve 3" silver **tight circles.** (Roll one of these circles on the center of quilling tool to allow space for jump ring.)

Assembly:
1. Glue shapes together, following pattern. Glue the tight circle with the larger hole in center and insert jump ring through it. Glue a tight circle on the points of the shaped teardrops in front and in back of jump ring.
2. Thread chain through jump ring. ∽

BEE & FLOWER PIN

Designed by Kathi Malarchuk Bailey

This charming bee and flower design makes a perfect accessory for springtime fashion.

MATERIALS

Quilling Paper:
1/8" wide
Black
Olive Green
Yellow

3/4" wide
Bright Blue
Light Blue

Other Supplies:
Quilling tool
Fringing tool
Pin back
Clear drying craft glue
Hot glue gun and glue sticks

INSTRUCTIONS

Bee (Make 1):
1. BODY (make 1): Lay a 12" yellow and a 12" black strip together. Using the two as one, make an **eccentric teardrop**.
2. WINGS (make 2): For each wing, roll a 12" black **eccentric circle**.
3. HEAD: (make 1): Roll a 3" black **loose circle**.
4. ANTENNAE: with a 1-1/2" strip of black, make a **V-scroll**.

Leaves (Make 3):
Make a 10" olive green **marquise** for each leaf.

Flower (Make 1):
Roll a bright blue and light blue **two-tone fringed flower** with a 12" strip of each color.

Assembly:
1. Glue bee parts, flower, and leaves together according to pattern. Let dry.
2. Hot-glue pin back to back of design. ∞

65

QUILLED HOME DECOR ACCESSORIES

From a welcome sign that has letters with the look of dried flowers to a boutique tissue box cover and much more, there are home accessories for all over the house in this collection of projects. There's a lampshade, decorator boxes, a personalized room sign, and even a quilled decorative egg. Treat yourself to a new bit of beauty for some spot in your home. You can easily make it yourself with the instructions given here.

WELCOME SIGN

Designed by Malinda Johnston

The appealing flowered letters of this welcome sign have the look of dried flowers and greenery, but they are made with quilling paper.

MATERIALS

Quilling Paper:
1/16" wide (or slit 1/8" wide paper)

Apricot	Coral	Gold
Green	Light Blue	Orange
Periwinkle Blue	Pink	Yellow

1/8" wide

Green	Lavender	Sage Green
Turquoise		

3/8" wide

Green	Sage Green

Other Supplies:
Quilling tool
Fringing tool
Fiberboard covered with dusty aqua shantung-look fabric, 18-5/8" x 4-7/8" x 1/8" thick
Gold frame to fit
Clear drying craft glue

INSTRUCTIONS

Bases of Letters:
Create the letters with 1/8" green paper on its edge. See the "L" shown in Fig. 1 as example. Create scrolls on the ends of the "L" and "C", allowing for these when you cut the length needed. The leaves, flowers, and greenery will be glued to these bases.

Leaves:
1. CUTOUT LEAVES: Cut out leaf shapes, varying the sizes, and curl them slightly. Wider leaves may be cut from 3/8" wide paper. Number of leaves needed are given in instructions for each letter below.
2. FRINGED LEAVES: Cut out leaf shapes, varying the sizes. Fringe leaves with scissors and curl them slightly. Wider leaves may be cut from 3/8" wide paper. Number of leaves needed are given in instructions for each letter below.

Continued on page 70

Welcome Sign

Pictured on page 68-69

continued from page 68

3. NARROW, CREASED LEAVES: Cut out leaf shapes and crease down the center. Some are straight, some of curved to fit the shape of the letter. Number of leaves needed are given in instructions for each letter below.
4. VARIEGATED LEAVES: Cut a leaf from one shade of green paper. Wider leaves may be cut from 3/8" wide paper. Cut a smaller leaf from a different shade of green and glue to first leaf. Number of leaves needed are given in instructions for each letter below.

Letter "W":

1. FLOWERS (make 3): Make three 2" orange **teardrops** as petals for each flower (9 total), using 1/16" paper. Glue petals together at an angle so that flower is cup-shaped. Roll a 1" apricot **tight circle** using 1/16" paper for each flower center (3 total) and glue to center of petals.
2. LEAVES: Make 15 green fringed leaves.
3. Glue flowers and leaves to letter base according to pattern.

First Letter "E":

1. FLOWERS (make 8): For each flower, make three 2" light blue **teardrops**, using 1/16" paper (9 total). These are petals. Glue petals together at an angle so the flower is cup-shaped. Roll a 1" periwinkle blue **tight circle**, using 1/16" paper for each flower center (3 total) and glue it in center of petals.
2. LEAVES: Cut 17 green fringed leaves.
3. Glue flowers and leaves to letter base according to pattern.

Letter "L":

1. FLOWERS (make 2): For each flower, make four 3" bright yellow **bunny ears** (8 total), using 1/8" paper. These are petals. Glue petals together at center, flat sides outward. Roll a 2" gold **loose circle**, using 1/16" paper, for each flower center (2 total). Glue in center to flower on top of petals.
2. LEAVES: Make five green fringed flowers.
3. TENDRILS (make 3): Make a 2" green **loose scrolls** for each tendril.
4. Glue flowers and leaves to letter base according to pattern.

Letter "C":

1. FLOWERS (make 3): For each flower, roll a coral **grape roll** (3 total), using 1/16" paper. Make one with a 5" length and two with a 6" length of paper.
2. LEAVES: Make 14 green fringed leaves.
3. TENDRILS (make 3): Make a short green **spiral**, using 1/16" paper for each.
4. Glue flowers, leaves, and tendrils to letter base according to pattern. (Glue smaller grape roll flower toward top end of the "C".)

Letter "O":

1. FLOWER (make 1): Make five 2" lavender **teardrops**, using 1/8" paper, for petals. Glue petals together in a circle, points inward. Roll three 1/2" yellow **loose scrolls**, using 1/16" paper. Glue scrolls in a cluster to center of flower.
2. BUDS (make 2): For each bud, make a 2" lavender **teardrop** (2 total), using 1/8" paper. For each calyx, make a 4" green **grape roll**, using 1/8" paper. Glue teardrop into grape roll.
3. LEAVES: Make 18 green cutout leaves.
4. Glue flowers and leaves to letter base according to pattern.

Letter "M":

1. FLOWERS (make 5): Make 3" turquoise **fringed flowers**, using 1/8" fringed paper.
2. LEAVES: Make 13 variegated leaves, using sage green on green.
3. TENDRILS (make 2): Make short green **spirals**, using 1/16" paper.
4. Glue flowers, leaves, and tendrils to letter base according to pattern.

Second Letter "E":

1. FLOWERS (make 9): For each flower, make a 3" **bunny ear** (9 total), using 1/8" paper.
2. LEAVES: Cut 17 green fringed leaves.
3. Glue flowers and leaves to letter base according to pattern.

Assembly:

1. Glue letters evenly spaced to fabric-covered board.
2. Secure board in frame. ∽

Fig. 1
Base of Letter "L"

ROSEBUD LAMPSHADE

Designed by Holly Witt

The quilled rosebud design on this little lamp adds an extra touch of brightness to any welcome.

MATERIALS

Quilling Paper, 1/8" wide:
Bright Yellow
Red
Seafoam Green

Other Supplies:
Quilling tool
Small white lampshade, 1-3/4" top
    diam. x 5" bottom diam. x 4" high
Welcome lamp
Clear drying craft glue

Pattern on page 74

INSTRUCTIONS

Top Border Squares (Make 21):
1. Make ten 5" seafoam green **squares.**
2. Make eleven 5" bright yellow **squares.**

Bottom Border Half Circles (Make 33):
1. Make 6" seafoam green loose circles.
2. Flatten one side of each for a **half circle.**

Dots (Make 14):
Roll a 2" bright yellow **tight circle** for each.

Rosebuds (Make 12):
Make a 4" red **teardrop** for each.

Leaves (Make 24):
Make a 4" seafoam green **teardrop** for each leaf.

Assembly:
1. Glue squares around top edge of lampshade, alternating colors.
2. Glue half circles around bottom edge of lampshade, flat sides downward.
3. Randomly glue rosebuds in an all-over pattern around lampshade according to pattern. Glue two leaves next to each rosebud.
4. Glue dots between rosebuds in an all-over pattern.
5. Place shade on welcome lamp. ❧

Rosebud Lampshade Pattern
Instructions & Photo on pages 72 & 73

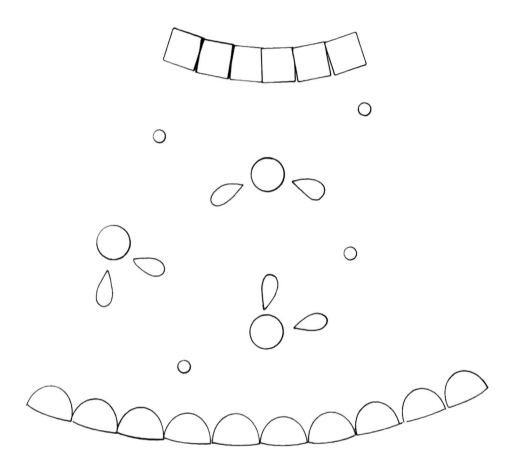

Repeat around lampshade

Flower Basket Tissue Box Pattern

Instructions and Photo on pages 76, 77

FLOWER BASKET TISSUE BOX COVER

Designed by Patty Cox

Why sit a plain old box of tissues out in full view? Make a lovely boutique tissue box holder with a quilled design – perfect for bedroom or bath.

MATERIALS

Quilling Paper, 1/8" wide, 5" lengths:
Off-white

Other Supplies:
Quilling tool
Clear acrylic boutique tissue box cover
Dark blue paper
Clear drying craft glue
Straight pins

Pattern on page 75

INSTRUCTIONS

Base Paper:
1. Cut the bottom from a box of tissues.
2. Wrap box with blue paper, gluing seams.
3. Cut out oval opening in top.
4. Fold and glue paper into bottom opening.

Corner Designs (Make 20):
1. Make one **eccentric loose circle** for each corner (20 total).
2. Make four **S-scrolls** for each corner (80 total)
3. Make one **diamond** for each corner (20 total).

Flowers (Make 12 – 3 for each side of box):
1. Roll one **tight circle** for each flower center (12 total).
2. Make five **eccentric loose circles** as petals for each flower (60 total).
3. Glue five petals around each flower center.

Leaves (Make 36 – 9 for each side of box):
For each leaf, make a **teardrop**.

Basket (Make 4 – 1 for each side of box):
1. Roll seven **loose circles** for each basket top.
2. Make 5 **triangles** for each basket middle.
3. Make 5 **squares** for each basket middle.
4. Roll five smaller **loose circles** for each basket bottom. These should measure 1/4" in diameter.

Assembly:
1. Arrange and glue a basket centered on each side of box according to pattern.
2. Arrange and glue a corner design in each corner of each box side and in each corner of box top, according to pattern. ୭୭

STACKED NATURE BOXES

Designed by Holly Witt

*Bugs can be beautiful. Consider the butterfly, the ladybug, and the bee.
These pretty creatures of nature are featured in quilled designs on these stackable
decorator boxes.*

MATERIALS

Quilling Paper, 1/8" wide:

Black	Bright Yellow
Light Blue	Purple
Red	Violet

Acrylic Craft Paints:

Light blue	Pale green
Pink	White
Yellow	

Other Supplies:

Quilling tool

Three papier mache round boxes with lids, 5" diam. x 2-3/4" high, and 4-1/4" diam. x 2" high, and 3-3/4" diam. x 1-3/4" high

1" flat brush

Matte varnish and foam brush

Clear drying craft glue

INSTRUCTIONS

Bee (Make 3):

1. WINGS (make 2 per bee – 6 total): Make 6" **teardrops.**
2. BODY (make 2 per bee – 6 total): Make 5" black **half circled** for top and bottom of each body.
3. STRIPE (make 1 per bee – 3 total): Make a 6" bright yellow **rectangle.**
4. ANTENNAE (make 2 per bee – 6 total): Make a 2" black **loose scroll** for each antenna.
5. Glue stripe between the top and bottom body. Glue a wing to each side of stripe. Glue two antenna to top of body.

Ladybug (Make 4):

1. BODY (make 2 per ladybug – 8

Ladybug – Make 4

Butterfly – Make 3

Bee – Make 3

total): Make an 8" red loose **half circle** for each side of each body.
2. HEAD (make 1 per ladybug – 4 total): Make a 5" black **half circle** for each head.
3. SPOTS (Make 6 per ladybug – 24 total): Roll a 2" black **tight circle** for each dot.
4. ANTENNAE (make 2 per ladybug – 8 total): Make a 1" black **loose scroll** for each antenna.
5. Glue loose ends of two antennae to rounded side of each ladybug head.

Butterflies (Make 3):

1. BODY (make 1 per butterfly – 3 total): Make a 4" light blue **teardrop** for each body.
2. HEAD (make 1 per butterfly – 3 total): Roll 4" a bright yellow **tight circle** for each head.
3. LARGE UPPER WINGS (make 2 per butterfly – 6 total): Make a 6" violet **teardrop** for each wing.
4. SMALL LOWER WINGS (make 2 per butterfly – 6 total): Make a 4" purple **teardrop** for each wing.
5. Glue each head to round end of each body. Glue wings to sides of each body with larger wings nearest head.

Assembly:

1. PAINT BOXES: Paint side of largest box with light blue and lid with yellow. Paint side of medium box with pale green and lid with white. Paint side of smallest box with pink and lid with light blue. Let dry.
2. Apply matte varnish to each box and lid and let dry.
3. Glue three bees to side of largest box. Cut little sections of black paper and glue to box for dash lines between bees.
4. Glue four ladybugs to side of medium box according to pattern. (Turn flat side of half circles toward each other for body). Glue three black tight circles on each half of each body for spots.
5. Glue three butterflies to side of smallest box. ✺

PERSONALIZED ROOM SIGN

Designed by Patty Cox

Children and teenagers love to label their space. Here's a great way for a little girl or young miss to beautifully say "This is my domain."

MATERIALS

Quilling Paper, 1/8" wide:
Green
Light blue
Pink
Yellow
Yellow Gold

Other Supplies:
Quilling tool
Lilac paper, 3-1/2" circle
Lavender paper, 3-1/2" circle
White paper, 2-3/4" circle
Two clear plastic round circles, 3"
Gold elastic cord, 4" long
Goldtone heart charm with keyhole, approx. 1/2"
Two goldtone head pins
Gold metallic wax
Pink permanent pen
Pinking shears
Clear drying craft glue

INSTRUCTIONS

Blue Birds (Make 2):
1. BODY (make 1 per bird – 2 total): Make an 8" light blue **teardrop** for each body.
2. WINGS (make 2 per bird – 4 total): Make a 6" light blue **teardrop** for each wing.
3. TAIL (make 1 per bird – 2 total): Make a 5" light blue **bunny ear** for each tail.
4. HEAD (make 1 per bird – 2 total): Roll a 5" light blue **loose circle** for each head.
5. BEAK (make 1 per bird – 2 total): Fold a small scrap of yellow gold paper in half. Trim ends to 1/8" long. Glue fold on head for beak.
6. Glue head, body, back wing, and tail together according to pattern. Glue front wing on top of body as shown on pattern.

Daffodils (Make 3):
1. TRUMPET (make 1 per daffodil – 3 total): Roll an 8" yellow loose circle for each trumpet. Pinch one side of each into **three points.**
2. LOWER PETALS (make 3 per flower – 9 total): Make a 5" yellow **teardrop** for each petal.
3. Glue rounded ends of three lower petals together and glue bottom of trumpet to center of petals according to pattern.

Leaves (Make 6):
Make a 5" green **teardrop** for each leaf.

Hearts (Make 3):
Make three pink **open hearts.**

Assembly:
1. Print name on white paper with the pink pen. Cut paper to a 2-3/4" circle.
2. Glue white paper on lavender paper. Trim lavender paper to a 3-1/8" circle. Glue on lilac paper. Trim lilac paper approximately 1/8" beyond lavender circle with pinking shears.
3. Glue quilled design on the white circle according to pattern.
4. Thread the gold cord through the top hole of one acrylic circle. *NOTE: If holes need to be added to acrylic circles, press holes with a T-pin that has been heated over the flame of a candle.* Tie ends together in a knot.
5. Place paper between the two clear acrylic circles, aligning holes. Insert head pins through holes, punching through paper layers. Bend the head pins on backside to secure the layers. Slide the heart charm on tail of bottom head pin.

FLORAL EGG

Designed by Patty Cox

Eggs are one of the most appealing shapes in nature, so naturally they are often decorated and used as home decorator accessories. Here's a unique egg, decorated with a quilled design.

MATERIALS

Quilling Paper, 1/8" wide, 5"
lengths:
Lavender
Pale yellow
Purple
Soft green
White

Other Supplies:
Quilling tool
Styrofoam® egg, 4"
Egg stand
Three large rubber bands
Clear drying craft glue
Spray matte finish

INSTRUCTIONS

Lavender Flowers (Make 14):
1. Roll a 5" pale yellow **tight circle** for each center (14 total)
2. Make five 5" lavender **bunny ears** for each flower (70 total).
3. Glue five lavender petals around each pale yellow flower center according to pattern.

White Flowers (Make 12):
1. Roll a 5" purple **tight circle** for each center (12 total).
2. Roll five 5" white **loose circles** for petals of each flower (60 total).
3. Glue five white petals around each purple flower center according to pattern.

Leaves (Make 42):
1. Make a 5" soft green **teardrop** for each leaf.
2. Glue three leaves to each lavender flower.

Background:
Roll 5" white **loose circles** – enough to fill in between flowers during assembly.

Assembly:
1. Cut the foam egg in half lengthwise.
2. Pin the quilled flowers around each half-egg. Fill in with white loose circles between flowers, also pinning these in place on the foam half-egg. Glue the shapes *to each other; avoid getting glue on the foam egg.* After glue has dried, lift each quilled half-egg away from the foam. Glue the halves together and secure with large rubber band until glue dries.
3. Spray egg with clear matte finish. ∞

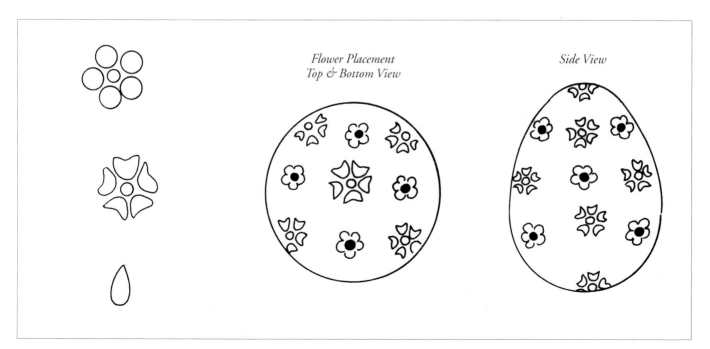

Flower Placement
Top & Bottom View

Side View

QUILLED PROJECTS FOR SPECIAL OCCASIONS

Special occasions or even specific seasons can be celebrated with flair by including some of these wonderful quilled projects. There are projects for bridal showers and baby showers, luminaries for fall or summer, and more. What is more deserving of the beautiful quilled additional touches than activities and events that were special to begin with? You'll love these ideas for making them better

KEEPSAKE BRIDAL SHOWER CAKE

Designed by Patty Cox

A lovely foam cake "frosted" with texturizing medium and acrylic paint and decorated with quilled flowers can set atop a real cake, then be kept and treasured as a remembrance of the wedding shower. Place it on the Keepsake Cake Plate project on pages 88 and 89.

Quilled Cake Decoration

MATERIALS

Quilling Paper, 1/8" wide, 5" lengths:
Lavender
Purple
Soft Green

Other Supplies:
Quilling tool
Clear drying craft glue
Straight pins

INSTRUCTIONS

Large Flowers (Make 18):
1. Roll a 5" purple **tight circle** for each flower center (18 total).
2. Make six 6" lavender **bunny ears** as petals for each large flower (108 total).
3. Glue six petals around a flower center for each large flower.

Small Flowers (Make 19):
1. Roll a 5" purple **tight circle** for each flower center (19 total).
2. Make three 6" lavender **bunny ears** as petals for each small flower (57 total).
3. Make a 6" soft green **bunny ear** for each small flower (19 total).
4. Glue three petals to one side of a flower center to make each small flower. Glue a soft green bunny ear on other side of each flower center.

Scrolls (Make 38):
Make 38 soft green **S-scrolls**.

Assembly:
Glue flowers and scrolls around sides of cake (upper and lower tiers), alternating large and small flowers with S-scrolls in between (see pattern and photo of project).

Cake to Decorate

MATERIALS

Two Styrofoam® disks: one 5-1/2" diam. x 2" thick, one 7-5/8" diam. x 2" thick
White acrylic paint or gesso
Texturizing medium
Lavender silk hydrangeas
Eleven white glittered plastic doves, approx. 1" long x 2" wide
Frosting knife
Three toothpicks
Sponge brush, 1"
Clear drying craft glue

INSTRUCTIONS

1. Stick three toothpicks into one flat surface of the smaller foam disk. Center it over the larger foam disk. Press disks together.
2. Frost "cake" with texturizing medium, using a frosting knife. Let dry.
3. Paint cake with white acrylic paint or gesso.
4. Glue quilled designs around cake sides. Secure designs with straight pins until dry.
5. Glue lavender silk hydrangeas on "cake" top. Decorate edges with glittered plastic doves. ∽

See page 89 for Keepsake Cake Plate instructions.

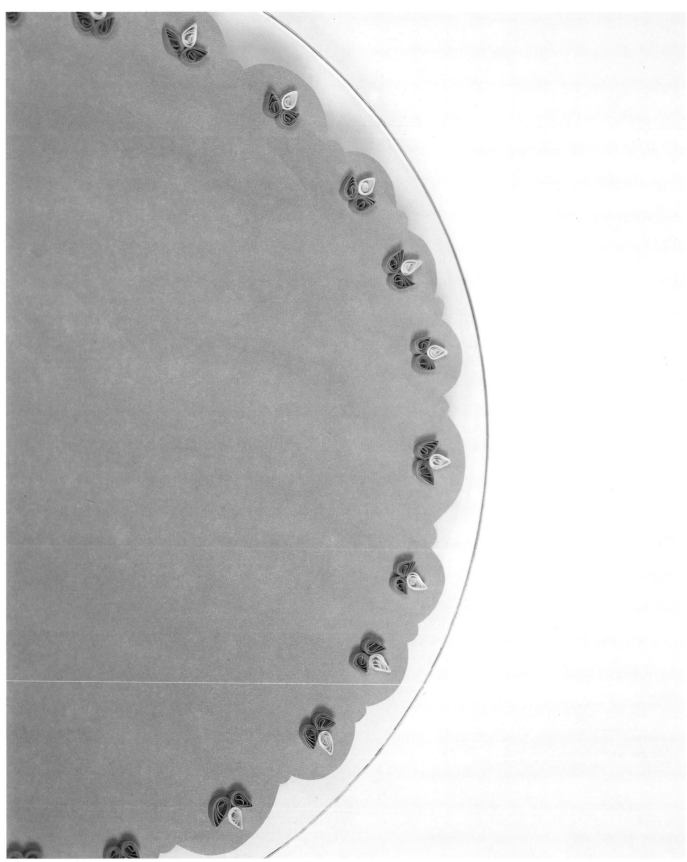

Closeup of Cake Plate

KEEPSAKE CAKE PLATE

Use this lovely cake plate with quilled design to hold the Keepsake Bridal Shower Cake project on pages 86 and 87.

MATERIALS

Quilling Paper, 1/8" wide, 2-1/2" lengths:
Soft Green
White

Other Supplies:
Quilling tool
Clear acrylic round cake plate, 10" diam.
Lavender round paper, 10" diam.
Scalloping edger scissors
Clear drying craft glue
Straight pins

INSTRUCTIONS

White Rosebuds (Make 24):
Make a 2-1/2" white **teardrop** for each rosebud.

Leaves (Make 48):
1. Make a 2-1/2" soft green **teardrop** for each leaf.
2. Glue two leaves under each rosebud.

Assembly:
1. Cut lavender paper to a 9-1/4" circle with scalloped edges, using scalloping scissors.
2. Glue a rosebud on each scallop.
3. Place decorated paper on clear acrylic cake plate. ∞

FALL LUMINARY

Designed by Holly Witt

MATERIALS

Quilling Paper, 1/8" wide:
Green
Gold
Rust

Other Supplies:
Quilling tool
Ivory handmade paper or rice
   paper, approx. 9-1/2" x 7-1/2"
Small hole punch
Clear drying craft glue

Pattern on page 92

INSTRUCTIONS

Acorns (Make 7):
1. Make a 6" gold **half circle** (with a slight point) for each acorn.
2. Make a 8" rust **half circle** for each acorn cap.
3. Fold a 1/4" strip of rust in half for each stem.

Oak Leaves (Make 2):
1. For each leaf, make three 8" green **teardrops** (top three leaves) and two 7" green **teardrops** for bottom two leaves.
2. Glue leaves on a 1-1/4" long strip of green paper for stem. Glue an 8" teardrop at very top and two 8" teardrops below that – one on each side of stem. Glue 7" teardrops below these – one on each side of stem.

Assembly:
1. Glue acorns and oak leaves on handmade or rice paper as shown in pattern.
2. Punch small holes in paper to allow more light to come through.
3. Roll paper into a cylinder, glue edge to secure cylinder, and place over a votive candle in a glass container. ∾

Fall Luminary Pattern

Instructions & Photo on pages 90 & 91

Summer Cookout Luminary Pattern

Instructions & Photo on pages 94 & 95

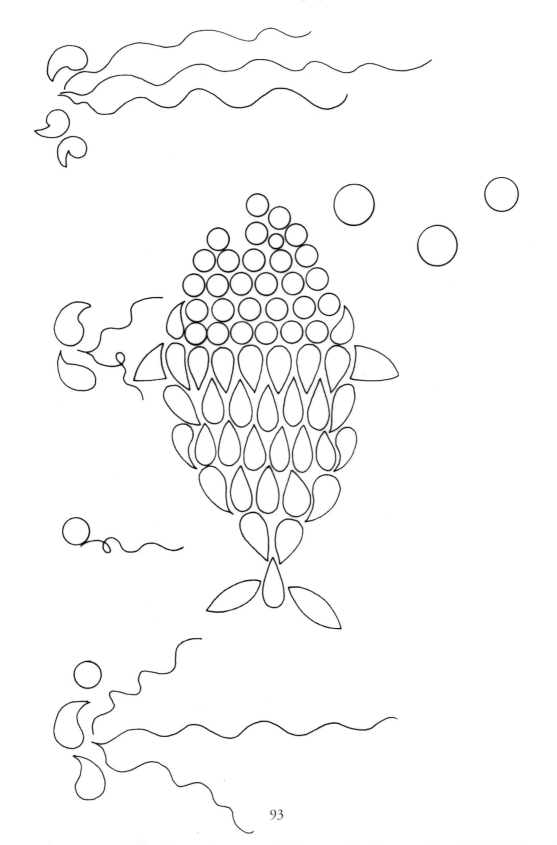

SUMMER COOKOUT LUMINARIA

Designed by Kathi Malarchuk Bailey

Whether it's by the beautiful sea or in your own backyard, a summer cookout gathering can have great style with one or more of these luminaries. It will add a festive atmosphere to a fun time.

MATERIALS

Quilling Paper, 1/8" wide:
Black
Bright Blue
Dark Green
Dark Orange
Dark Purple
Light Blue
Light Green
Medium Green
Orange
White
Yellow

Other Supplies:
Quilling tool
Blue parchment paper, 8-1/2" x 11" sheet
Clear drying craft glue

Pattern on page 93

INSTRUCTIONS

Fish (Make 1):

1. HEAD: Roll ten 6" yellow **loose circles**. Roll eighteen 6" orange **loose circles**. Roll two 6" dark orange **loose circles**.

2. EYE: Roll a 1-1/2" black **tight circle**.

3. BODY: Make seven 8" bright blue **teardrops**. Make eleven 8" light blue **teardrops**. Make eight 8" light green **teardrops**. Make three 8" dark green **teardrops**.

4. TAIL: Make two 8" dark green **marquises**.

5. FINS (make 2): For each fin, make an 8" dark green **triangle**.

6. Glue quilled shapes together according to fish pattern.

Seaweed (Make 13):
Make the following **loose spirals**:

one 6" medium green   one 6" light green
three 4" medium green   three 4" light green
five 3" light green

Shells (Make 7)

1. Make one each color of dark green, bright blue, and purple 8" shaped teardrops (3 total).

2. Make four 8" white **shaped teardrops**.

Bubbles (Make 3):

1. Make two 8" white **loose circles**.
2. Make one 6" white **loose circles**.

Assembly:

1. Cut parchment down to 5-1/2" x 11". Cut top edge (an 11" edge) into an irregular wave pattern.

2. Glue quilled design centered on parchment according to the pattern. Let dry thoroughly.

3. Roll and glue short ends together to make a luminary cylinder. ∽

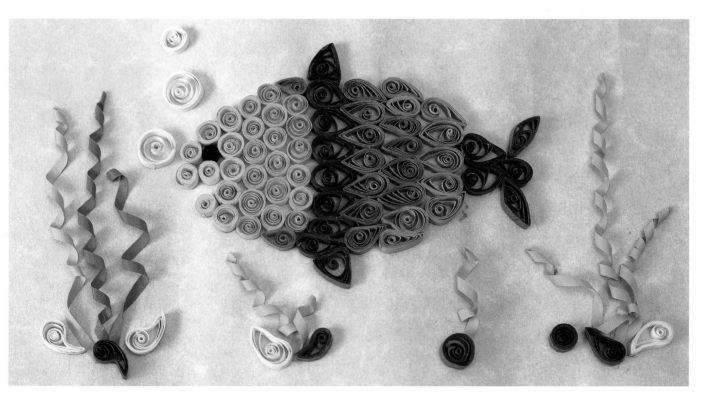

MEMENTO ALBUM PAGE

Sometimes mementos are dimensional, and sometimes even flat mementos like photos, announcements, or invitations deserve extra frills that may be dimensional. Keepsake album pages with "bubbles" will keep them safe and beautiful.

MATERIALS

Quilling Paper, 1/8" wide:
Bright Pink
Light Pink
Olive Green
Yellow

Other Supplies:
Quilling tool
Keepsake album page with "bubble" areas, 8-1/2" x 11"
Keepsake items (shown are wedding photo, wedding invitation, and dried wedding flowers)
Yellow parchment, 8-1/2" x 11" sheet
Clear drying craft glue

INSTRUCTIONS

Flowers (Make 2:
1. For each flower, make four 12" light pink **teardrops** (8 total) for petals.
2. For each flower center, roll three 1-1/2" yellow **tight circles** (6 total).
3. For each flower, glue four teardrops together in a circle, points inward. Glue three tight circles on center of each flower.

Leaves (Make 5 Large & 3 Small):
1. Make a 12" olive green **marquise** for each large leaf.
2. Make a 6" olive green **marquise** for each small leaf.

Three-Petal Bud (Make 1):
1. Make three 6" bright pink **teardrops.**
2. Glue teardrops together in a half circle, points toward center bottom.

Large Single Bud (Make 1):
Make an 8" bright pink **teardrop.**

Bee (Make 1):
1. BODY: Place a 12" length of yellow paper and a 12" length of black paper together and treat as one. With yellow outward, roll an **eccentric circle.**
2. WING: Roll a 12" black **eccentric circle.**
3. HEAD: Roll a 5" black **tight circle.**
4. ANTENNAE: Cut a 1" strip of black paper. Crease in middle. Roll both ends slightly in the same direction.
5. Glue parts of bee together as shown in photo.

Vines (Make 2 Large & 3 Small):
1. Make a 5" olive green **loose scroll** for each large vine.
2. Make a 1-1/2" olive green **loose scroll** for each small vine.

Scrolls (Make 7):
Roll a 6" olive green **loose scroll** for each.

Assembly:
1. Using white backing paper from album page as a template, cut a new backing from yellow parchment. Retain white backing for "bubble" insert areas.
2. Glue mementos (photos, invitation, etc.) to backing for appropriate "bubble" areas, reserving the vertical oval area for quilled design.
3. Glue floral quilled design to backing of oval insert area according to the pattern.
4. Glue bud, one small leaf, bee, and scrollwork to album page around "bubbles" as shown in photo of project. ∽

Kathleen Malarchuk
and
E. Bart Bailey
te you to share in the joy o
our Wedding
turday, the third of Octo
en hundred and ninety eig
t twelve o'clock noon

BABY SHOWER DECORATIONS

Celebrate the infancy or the emerging childhood of the newborn at a baby shower that uses this charming quilled frame or adorable teddy bear as favors. The new mother or mother-to-be will treasure them.

Childhood Frame
Design by Betty Christy

MATERIALS

Quilling Paper, 1/8" wide:
Pink

Other Supplies:
Quilling tool (slotted tool recommended)
Ivory matboard heart shaped frame with heart shape opening, 4-1/2" x 5" with 2-1/2" x 3" opening
Black silhouette cutout of little girl with doll, approx. 1-1/2" x 1-3/4"
Permanent ink pens: black, green
Clear drying craft glue

INSTRUCTIONS

Roses (Make 10):
Make ten pink **folded roses.**

Assembly:
1. Glue silhouette in center of cutout area.
2. Draw vine around frame with black and green permanent pens according to pattern.
3. Glue nine folded roses on vine around top and sides and one at the bottom point as shown in photo of project. ∞

How to Make Folded Roses

Slip the end of the paper strip into the slot of a slotted quilling tool. Begin rolling the strip to make the center of the flower. Next, fold the paper away from you at a right angle. Roll the paper again, keeping the bottom edge tight on the tool and allowing the top edge to flare outward. Continue rolling until the fold is on the top. Make another right-angle fold. Roll the paper again, allowing it to flare out. Repeat the folding and rolling steps until the entire strip has been shaped or until the rose is the desired size. Glue end of strip in place.

Teddy Bear Shower Favor
Designed by Kathi Malarchuk Bailey

MATERIALS

Quilling Paper:
1/8" wide
Black
Light Lavender
3/8" wide
Bright Blue

Other Supplies:
Quilling tool
Fringing tool
Bright blue paper square, 3"
Clear plastic cupcake "poke"
Clear drying craft glue

INSTRUCTIONS

Bear (Make 1):
1. BODY & HEAD: Make seventeen 6" **fringed "flowers"**, using bright blue fringed paper.
2. EYES: Roll a 1-1/2" black **tight circle** for each eye (2 total).
3. BOW: Cut two 1-1/2" strips of lavender paper. Form loops from one strip and streamers and wrap from other strip (for wrap, turn the upper end of one streamer over front of loops). Glue bow pieces together.

Assembly:
1. Glue 16 fringed "flowers" together to form bear's body according to the pattern, turning fringed sides forward. (Omit fringed "flower" in center of head for now.) Let glue dry thoroughly.

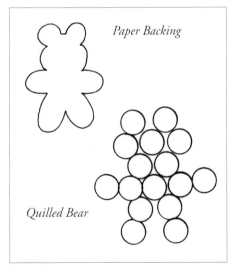

Paper Backing

Quilled Bear

2. Add remaining fringed "flower" to front of head for muzzle, turning fringed side forward (same as

Continued on next page

Teddy Bear Shower Favor (cont.)
    others) but let it extend forward approximately 1/4" further than others.
3. Flare out fringes of all "flowers."
4. Glue black eyes in place on head.
5. Glue bow to neck (under muzzle).
6. Glue teddy bear to the top end of a plastic cupcake "poke."
7. Cut bear shape from paper according to the pattern. Glue it over plastic
    "poke" and to back of bear. Insert favor in cupcake. ∞

Miniature Green House

Designed by Betty Christy

This is what you do with all your paper scraps. It isn't exactly a "quilling" project but it is an extension of the skills learned for quilling. Betty created this miniature greenhouse using dollhouse miniatures that are 1 to 10 scale. Use your imagination to create a similar piece.

All the flowers and greenery were made with quilling paper. The "clay pots" are made with pieces of orange or white 1/8" quilling paper, using the entire 24" length. Use the grape roll technique to shape them into a pot.

The sides of the greenhouse are pieces of 1/16" thick plexiglas that have been framed with stained pieces of 3/8" and 1/8" wide balsa wood strips. The 3/8" strips are glued on top of the glas piece and all around the perimeter of the piece. The 1/8" strips are placed vertically across the pieces. Following are the measurements for the greenhouse sides.

Bottom: 8" x 11-3/4" (this is a solid piece of 1/8" thick bass wood. The top surface is covered with 1/4" wide pieces of stained balsa wood to look like floorboards.

Roof pieces (2): 11-3/4" x 6"

Sides (2): 11-3/4" x 4"

Front & Back: 8-1/4" wide, 8" high at peak, and 4" high at sides

CHRISTMAS QUILLING

Happy holidays are even happier when
you make some of the decorations yourself,
and even prettier with these quilled designs.
Ornaments for the tree or wall, a decorator
box to hold your cards or other items,
quilled angels and snowflakes, winter-theme
gift tags, even an exquisite cathedral – here's
a bonanza of creativity and Christmas cheer!

POINSETTIA BALL ORNAMENT

Designed by Patty Cox

Make your own special Christmas tree balls. This poinsettia design is just one of many ways you can add your own quilled beauty to your tree.

MATERIALS

Quilling Paper, 1/8" wide, 5" lengths:
Green
Red
Yellow Gold

Other Supplies:
Quilling tool
Papier mache ball, 2-1/2"
Gold cord, 3" long
Clear drying craft glue
Spray matte finish

INSTRUCTIONS

Poinsettias (Make 12):
1. Roll a yellow gold **tight circle** for each flower center (12 total)
2. For each flower, make five red **teardrops** (60 total) for petals.
3. For each flower, make five green **teardrops** (60 total) for leaves.
4. Glue five petals around each flower center. Glue five green leaves between petals as shown on pattern.

Background:
Roll green **loose circles** – enough to fill in background between poinsettias.

Assembly:
1. Glue poinsettias evenly spaced around the paper mache ball.
2. Fill in between poinsettias with green loose circles until entire background is covered. Let glue dry.
3. Glue a gold cord to top of ball for a hanger. ∽

FRAMED SNOWFLAKE

Designed by Patty Cox

There seems to be a sort of magic about snowflakes. But you can't keep the ones that fall from the sky. Quill and frame a remembrance of a favorite winter day.

MATERIALS

Quilling Paper, 1/8" wide:
White

Other Supplies:
Quilling tool
White frame, 9" x 9"
Metallic blue paper – piece to fit inside frame (approx. 8" square) and 5-3/4" square
White paper, 6-1/4" square
White translucent parchment or wax paper, same size as larger metallic blue paper
Scissors for decorative edging
Heart paper punch
Package clear AB acrylic beads, assorted sizes 2mm to 6mm
Clear drying craft glue
Glue stick
Straight pins

Pattern on page 108

INSTRUCTIONS

Base Paper
1. Cut a 5-5/8" square of metallic blue paper, using decorative edger scissors. Punch a heart in each corner with the heart punch.
2. Center and glue (with glue stick) metallic blue square onto a 6-1/4" white square trimmed with decorative edger scissors.
3. Cover larger metallic blue paper with same size translucent parchment or wax paper. Center and glue (with glue stick) trimmed white and blue squares onto this.

Loose Circles (Make 32):
Roll 32 white **loose circles.**

Marquises (Make 20):
Make twenty white **marquises.**

Teardrops (Make 4):
Make twenty white **teardrops.**

Open Hearts (Make 24):
Make 24 white **open hearts.**

Assembly:
1. Arrange and glue circles, marquises, teardrops, and hearts on the center metallic blue paper according to pattern.
2. Glue clear acrylic beads in center of scrolled areas, in center of snowflake, and between quilled design as shown in photo of project. ∾

Framed Snowflake Pattern

Instructions & Photo on pages 106 & 107

Snowflake Box

Instructions & Photo on pages 110 & 111

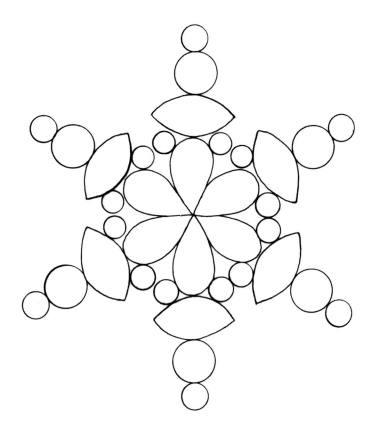

SNOWFLAKE BOX

Designed by Malinda Johnston

Perfect for holding Christmas cards or small Christmas gift trinkets for guests,
this box is decorated with the prettiest symbol of wintertime – the snowflake.

MATERIALS

Quilling Paper, 1/8" wide:
White

Other Supplies:
Quilling tool
Fabric-covered lidded papier mache
box (beige crushed velvet shown),
7-5/8" x 5-3/4" x 3-3/4" deep
Red cardstock, 5" square
Gold/red braid
Clear drying craft glue

Pattern on page 109

INSTRUCTIONS

Snowflake (Make 1):
1. Make the following white quilled shapes:
   Six 9" **eccentric teardrops**
   Six 9" **eccentric fans**
   Six 6" **eccentric circles**
   Eighteen 3" **eccentric circles**
2. Glue shapes into snowflake design according to pattern. Start in the center and work outward.

Assembly:
1. Center and glue the red cardstock square on top of box lid.
2. Glue braid around edges of red square.
3. Center and glue the quilled snowflake on the red square. ∞

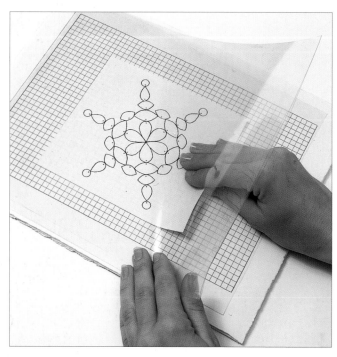

CHRISTMAS ANGEL SHADOWBOX

Designed by Patty Cox

*Here's a quilled angel adorned with holly and displayed in a shadowbox to
add dimensional beauty to your wall during the holidays.*

MATERIALS

Quilling Paper, 1/8" wide:
Green
Ivory
Red

Other Supplies:
Quilling tool
Shadowbox, 5-1/4" x 7-1/2" (4-3/8" x 7-1/4" rabbet measurement)
Green corrugated paper, 4-3/8" x 7-1/4" or size to fit back of shadowbox
Corrugated cardboard, 2-1/2" x 4"
Metallic gold paper
Red handmade paper
Foam core board
Goldtone bell, approx. 5/8"
Antique white acrylic craft paint
Metallic gold paint
Paint brush
Sponge
Clear drying craft glue
Tweezers

Pattern on page 114

INSTRUCTIONS

Angel:
1. WINGS: Make sixteen 5" ivory **teardrops.**
2. TORSO: Make two 5" ivory **squares.**
3. SKIRT: Make 53, 5" ivory **teardrops.** Glue teardrops together in groups of three as shown in Fig. 1 to make scallops. Make fifteen scallops for skirt. Remaining teardrops will be used singly.
4. HEAD: Roll a 12" ivory **eccentric circle** for head.
5. Glue wings, body, skirt, and head together according to pattern.

Corners (Make 4):
1. Make twelve 5" ivory **teardrops.**
2. Glue teardrops into four sets of three, as you did for skirt scallops (Fig. 1).

Holly:
1. BERRIES: Roll six 5" red **tight circles.**
2. LEAVES: Make eight 5" green **holly leaves.** Use tweezers to sharply crease points.
3. Assemble two holly sprigs – one for head and one for skirt – according to patterns.
4. Glue the five-leaf holly sprig to top of head. Glue the three-leaf sprig on skirt.

Arms & Bell:
1. Cut a 3" length of ivory quilling paper. Thread bell on center of length.
2. Apply glue to each end of the paper length. Slide paper ends through top torso square to body back. These positions are shown on pattern. Pull paper through to desired length. Trim and glue paper ends on body back.

Assembly:
1. Paint shadowbox with antique white. Let dry. Sponge face and outer sides of box with metallic gold. Let dry.
2. Glue green corrugated paper in back of shadowbox.
3. Glue angel on the 2-1/4" x 4" piece of corrugated cardboard. Glue cardboard to metallic gold paper. Tear edges of gold paper 1/8" larger all around than the corrugated cardboard. Glue gold paper on red handmade paper. Tear edges of red paper 1/4" larger all around than gold paper. Glue red paper on a 2-7/8" x 4-1/8" piece of foam core board. Glue foam core board on a piece of metallic gold paper torn to 3-3/8" x 4-7/8". Glue this gold paper on a 3-1/4" x 4-3/4" piece of foam core board. Cut a smaller piece of foam core board and glue on back of all layers. Center and glue layers in shadowbox.
4. Glue quilled corners in each corner of shadowbox approximately 1/4" back from where glass will be. Secure these with straight pins until dry.
5. Place and secure glass in shadowbox. ∞

Fig. 1

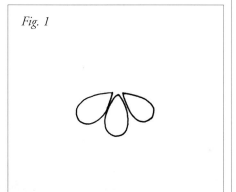

Christmas Angel Shadowbox Pattern

Instructions & Photo on pages 112 & 113

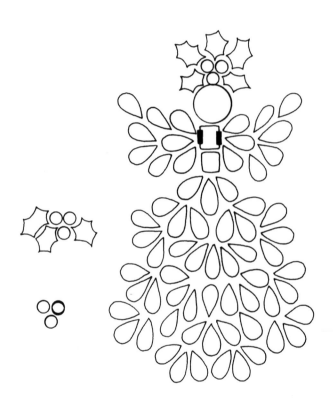

Ornament Display Box Pattern

Instructions & Photo on pages 116 & 117

ORNAMENT DISPLAY BOX

Designed by Patty Cox

*When you have a favorite ornament, especially one that no longer fits
your tree theme or which you don't want to risk getting broken on the tree,
here's the perfect way to display it safely during the holidays – in a shadowbox
on the wall.*

MATERIALS

**Quilling Paper, 1/8" wide, 5"
  lengths:**
Pale pink

Other Supplies:
Quilling tool
Shadowbox, 6-5/8" x 8-5/8" (5-1/8"
  x 7-1/8" rabbet measurement)
Navy mat to fit frame with 3" x 4"
  oval opening
Pale pink paper, 5" x 7"
Two strips foam core board, 1/2" x 7"
22 off-white 3mm or 4mm beads
Antique white acrylic craft paint
Paint brush
Craft knife
Flexible industrial glue
Clear drying craft glue

Pattern on page 115

INSTRUCTIONS

Quilled Border:
1. Make 24, 5" **S-scrolls.**
2. Make ten 5" **eccentric teardrops.**
3. Make two 2-1/2" **teardrops**
4. Arrange and glue quilled pieces to navy mat around oval opening according
   to pattern.

Assembly:
1. Glue off-white beads between quilled pieces as shown in photo of project.
2. Paint shadowbox antique white.
3. Glue a 5" x 7" piece of pale pink paper in back of shadowbox.
4. Glue 1/2" x 7" strips of foam core board on each inner side of box. These
   will lift the mat 1/2" forward from the background paper.
5. Glue decorated mat on edges of foam core board strips in box.
6. Stack and glue three 1-1/2" square of foam core board together. Carve the
   top edge into a rounded end, using a craft knife.
7. With flexible industrial glue, glue the ornament to the rounded end of the
   foam core board stack. Glue opposide flat end to back of box (on the pink
   paper). ∽

CHRISTMAS CATHEDRAL

Designed by Patty Cox

*The majesty of a real cathedral with its beautiful stained glass windows is
captured in this table decoration. It looks so exquisite, yet it is quite easy to make.*

MATERIALS

Quilling Paper, 1/8" wide:
Black
Ivory
Red
Turquoise
Yellow Gold

Other Supplies:
Quilling tool
Foam core board
Black craft acrylic paint
Silver spray paint
Copper paper
Metallic gold paper
Paint brush
Three round red frosted cabachons
Goldtone bell, approx. 3/4"
Craft knife
Clear drying craft glue

Patterns on pages 120, 121

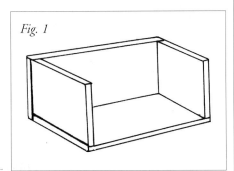

Fig. 1

INSTRUCTIONS

Foam Core Board Cathedral:
1. Using patterns, cut cathedral parts from foam core board with a craft knife. Cut out circles, arched (gothic) window shapes, and rectangular door shapes from the three gothic shapes as shown on patterns.
2. Glue the three gothic shapes on foam core background piece for cathedral front.
3. Make enough 5" ivory **teardrops** and **S-scrolls** to cover front of cathedral wall around cutout areas. Let glue on pieces dry.
4. Spray foam core board pieces and wall quilling with silver spray paint. Let dry.

Doors:
1. Cut two 7/8" x 2" pieces of copper paper for doors. Glue in position to background foam core cathedral front behind cutout doors.
2. Make four 5" ivory **triangles** for hinges.
3. Make two 5" ivory **S-scrolls** for door trim.
4. Glue hinges and trim on doors as shown on pattern.

Large Rose Window (Make 1):
1. Make twenty-four 2-1/2" yellow gold **teardrops.**
2. Roll nine 2-1/2" yellow gold **tight circles.**
3. Make eight 2-1/2" red **marquises.**
4. Make 48, 2-1/2" red **teardrops.**
5. Roll sixteen 2-1/2" red **tight circles.**
6. Make 72, 2-1/2" black **teardrops.**
7. Roll 32, 2-1/2" turquoise **tight circles.**
8. Make 32, 2-1/2" turquoise **teardrops.**
9. Secure one yellow gold tight circle in center of work with a straight pin. Glue rounds of other shapes together according to pattern.
10. Glue in large round cutout area of cathedral front (middle gothic piece).

Small Rose Windows (Make 2):
1. For each small rose window, complete the first four rows of the large rose window, ending with the turquoise/black row.
2. Glue in small round cutout areas of cathedral front (side gothic pieces).

Gothic Windows (Make 2):
1. Cut two metallic gold paper shapes according to arched window pattern. Glue paper in position to background board behind cutout arched windows.
2. Glue red cabachons at top of window shapes as shown on pattern.
3. For each window, make four 2-1/2" black **teardrops.**
4. For each window, make eight 5" black **squares.**
5. Glue quilled pieces in position in each gothic window according to pattern.

Continued on page 120

Christmas Cathedral Patterns

Instructions & Photo on pages 118 & 119

Large Rose Window

Continued from page 118

Bell Window:
1. Paint background board inside small circular bell window with black acrylic paint. Let dry.
2. Attach bell through foam core board at top of this cutout area.

Cathedral Backing Box:
1. Cut the following pieces from foam core board:
   Bottom – 3-3/4" x 8-5/8"
   Two sides – 3-3/4" x 4-1/2"
   Back – 8-5/8" x 4-5/8"
2. Glue backing box together as shown in Fig. 1. Hold sections together with straight pins until glue dries. (The height of the box is 4-5/8".)
3. Glue backing box to back of cathedral front. ∞

Circle Guide for Rose Window (place under wax paper on quilling board)

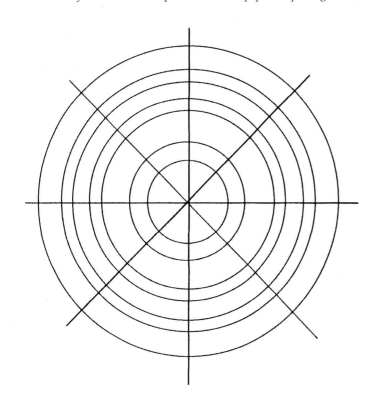

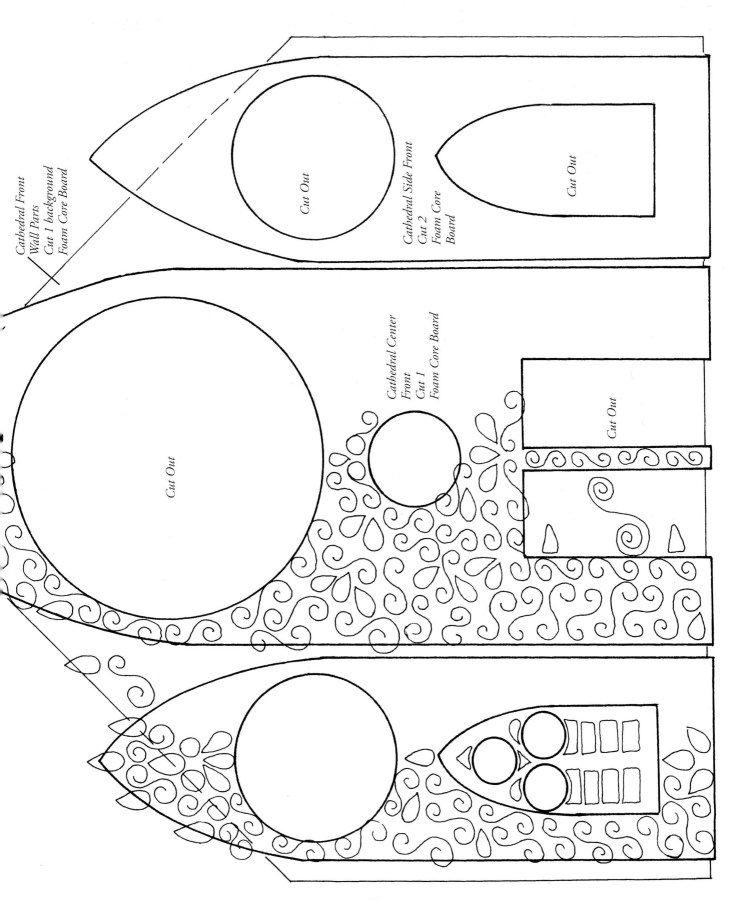

Cathedral Front
Wall Parts
Cut 1 background
Foam Core Board

Cut Out

Cathedral Side Front
Cut 2
Foam Core
Board

Cut Out

Cathedral Center
Front
Cut 1
Foam Core Board

Cut Out

Cut Out

Cut Out

CHRISTMAS GIFT TAGS
Designed by Holly Witt

Write your Christmas message on the back of a quilled tag and tie it on a special gift. They will know you care.

Tree Of My Heart

MATERIALS

Quilling Paper, 1/8" wide:
Bright Green
Red
Rust
Yellow

Other Supplies:
Quilling tool
Scrap of black/white patterned fabric
Tagboard, 2-1/2" x 4"
White tagboard, 2" x 3-1/2"
Fusible webbing
Black permanent marker
Paper punch
Pinking shears
Clear drying craft glue

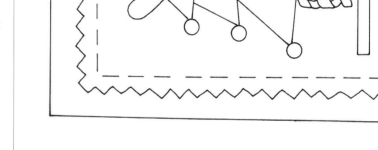

INSTRUCTIONS

Tree (Make 1:)
1. Make a 5", a 7", and a 9" **bright green** triangle.
2. Glue together, one above the other, the smallest on top and largest on bottom (see pattern).
3. Make a 1" rust **spiral** and glue to center bottom of tree for trunk.

Ornaments (Make 6):
1. Make a 2" yellow **semi-loose circle** for each ornament.
2. Glue ornaments to lower points of triangles on both sides of tree.

Heart (Make 1):
1. Make an 8" red **heart (arrow)**.
2. Glue to top of tree.

Grass:
Accordion fold a 3" length of bright green for grass.

Assembly:
1. Iron black/white fabric to tagboard, using fusible webbing.
2. Trim white tagboard piece with pinking shears. Center and glue to front of patterned fabric.
3. Punch hole in top of tag with paper punch.
4. Draw running stitch marks around edge of white tagboard with a black marker.
5. Glue tree and grass to white tagboard as shown on pattern. ∞

Santa Cheer

MATERIALS

Quilling Paper, 1/8" wide:
Flesh
Red
White
Yellow

Other Supplies:
Quilling tool
Scrap of red/white pindot fabric
Tagboard, 2-1/2" x 4"
Green tagboard, 2" x 3-1/2"
Fusible webbing

Black permanent marker
Paper punch
Pinking shears
Clear drying craft glue

continued on next page

Santa Cheer

Pictured on page 123

continued from page 123

INSTRUCTIONS

Santa Head (Make 1):
1. Make a 6" flesh **rectangle** for face.
2. Make two 2" white **squares** for side-burns and glue to each side of face.
3. Make a 10" white **half circle** for beard and glue to bottom of face.
4. Make two 5" white **shaped teardrops** for mustache and glue on top of upper beard below face.
5. Make two 1" black **tight circles** for eyes and glue on face.
6. Make a 4" red **tight circle** for nose and glue on top of mustache at center.

Santa Hat (Make 1):
1. Make an 8" red **triangle** for hat.
2. Make an 8" white **rectangle** for hat cuff and glue to bottom of hat.
3. Make a 2" white **tight circle** for pom-pon and glue to top tip of hat.
4. Make a 3" yellow **crescent** and glue to front of hat for decoration.
5. Glue hat to top of Santa's head.

Collar (Make 1):
1. Roll four 4" red **loose circles** for collar.

2. Glue circles side by side to bottom of Santa's beard.

Assembly:
1. Iron pindot fabric to tagboard, using fusible webbing.
2. Trim green tagboard piece with pinking shears. Center and glue to front of pindot fabric.
3. Punch hole in top of tag with paper punch.
4. Draw running stitch marks around edge of green tagboard with a black marker.
5. Glue Santa to green tagboard as shown on pattern.
6. Cut out little squares from white paper for confetti snowflakes and glue to green background. ∾

Happy Snowman

Pictured on page 125

MATERIALS

Quilling Paper, 1/8" wide:

Black	Orange	Red
Rust	White	

Other Supplies:
Quilling tool
Scrap of red/white gingham fabric
Tagboard, 2-1/2" x 4"
Fusible webbing
Bright blue paper, 2" x 3-1/2"
Black permanent marker
Paper punch
Clear drying craft glue

INSTRUCTIONS

Snowman (Make 1):
1. Roll a 4", a 6", and an 8" white **loose circle** for body/head.
2. Glue together, one on top of the other, the smallest on top and largest on bottom (see pattern).

Arms (Make 2):
1. For each arm, bend a 2" length of rust paper in half (part of which will be the middle finger. Fold a finger on each side of middle finger as shown in pattern.
2. Glue an arm on each side of body.

Facial Features:
1. EYES (make 2): Roll a 1" black **tight circle** for each eye.
2. NOSE: Make a 3" orange long **triangle** for nose.
3. Glue facial features to head.

continued on next page

Happy Snowman (cont.)

Hat (Make 1):

1. Make a 7" black **square** for hat crown.
2. Glue a small strip of white paper across hat crown at bottom for hat band.
3. Accordion-fold a 1-1/2" strip of black paper for hat brim.
4. Glue hat pieces together, then glue on top of snowman's head.

Heart (Make 1):

1. Make an 8" red **heart (arrow)**.
2. Glue to front of snowman body.

Snowflakes (Make 10):

Roll a 1" white **tight circle** for each snowflake.

Assembly:

1. Iron gingham fabric to tagboard, using fusible webbing.
2. Center and glue bright blue paper to front of gingham fabric.
3. Punch hole in top of tag with paper punch.
4. Draw blanket stitch marks around edge of blue paper with a black marker.
5. Glue snowman to blue paper as shown on pattern.
6. Glue snowflakes on the blue background around snowman. ∽

METRIC CONVERSION

INCHES TO MILLIMETERS AND CENTIMETERS

Inches	MM	CM
1/8	3	.3
1/4	6	.6
3/8	10	1.0
1/2	13	1.3
5/8	16	1.6
3/4	19	1.9
7/8	22	2.2
1	25	2.5
1-1/4	32	3.2
1-1/2	38	3.8
1-3/4	44	4.4
2	51	5.1
3	76	7.6
4	102	10.2
5	127	12.7
6	152	15.2
7	178	17.8
8	203	20.3
9	229	22.9
10	254	25.4
11	279	27.9
12	305	30.5

YARDS TO METERS

Yards	Meters
1/8	.11
1/4	.23
3/8	.34
1/2	.46
5/8	.57
3/4	.69
7/8	.80
1	.91
2	1.83
3	2.74
4	3.66
5	4.57
6	5.49
7	6.40
8	7.32
9	8.23
10	9.14

Index

INDEX